Six Sigma Marketing

From Cutting Costs to
Growing Market Share

Also available from ASQ Quality Press:

Competing for Customers and Winning with Value: Breakthrough Strategies for Market Dominance
R. Eric Reidenbach and Reginald W. Goeke

Strategic Six Sigma for Champions: Keys to Sustainable Competitive Advantage
R. Eric Reidenbach and Reginald W. Goeke

Value-Driven Channel Strategy: Extending the Lean Approach
R. Eric Reidenbach and Reginald W. Goeke

Managing the Customer Experience: A Measurement-Based Approach
Morris Wilburn

Proving Continuous Improvement with Profit Ability
Russ Jones

The Executive Guide to Understanding and Implementing Lean Six Sigma: The Financial Impact
Robert M. Meisel, Steven J. Babb, Steven F. Marsh, and James P. Schlichting

Transactional Six Sigma for Green Belts: Maximizing Service and Manufacturing Processes
Samuel E. Windsor

Lean Kaizen: A Simplified Approach to Process Improvements
George Alukal and Anthony Manos

Root Cause Analysis: Simplified Tools and Techniques, Second Edition
Bjørn Andersen and Tom Fagerhaug

The Certified Manager of Quality/Organizational Excellence Handbook: Third Edition
Russell T. Westcott, editor

Enabling Excellence: The Seven Elements Essential to Achieving Competitive Advantage
Timothy A. Pine

To request a complimentary catalog of ASQ Quality Press publications, call 800-248-1946, or visit our Web site at www.asq.org/quality-press.

Six Sigma Marketing

From Cutting Costs to Growing Market Share

R. Eric Reidenbach

ASQ Quality Press
Milwaukee, Wisconsin

American Society for Quality, Quality Press, Milwaukee 53203

© 2009 by American Society for Quality

All rights reserved. Published 2009

Printed in the United States of America

15 14 13 12 11 10 09   5 4 3 2 1

Library of Congress Cataloging-in-Publication Data

Reidenbach, R. Eric.

Six sigma marketing: from cutting costs to growing market share / Eric Reidenbach.

p. cm.

Includes bibliographical references and index.

ISBN 978-0-87389-768-6 (alk. paper)

1. Marketing—Management.   2. Marketing—Quality control.   3. Six sigma. (Quality control standard)   I. Title.

HF5415.13.R368 2009

658.8'02—dc22

2009007648

Publisher: William A. Tony

Acquisitions Editor: Matt Meinholz

Project Editor: Paul O'Mara

Production Administrator: Randall Benson

ASQ Mission: The American Society for Quality advances individual, organizational, and community excellence worldwide through learning, quality improvement, and knowledge exchange.

Attention Bookstores, Wholesalers, Schools, and Corporations: ASQ Quality Press books, videotapes, audiotapes, and software are available at quantity discounts with bulk purchases for business, educational, or instructional use. For information, please contact ASQ Quality Press at 800-248-1946, or write to ASQ Quality Press, P.O. Box 3005, Milwaukee, WI 53201-3005.

To place orders or to request a free copy of the ASQ Quality Press Publications Catalog, including ASQ membership information, call 800-248-1946. Visit our Web site at www.asq.org or http://www.asq.org/quality-press.

♾ Printed on acid-free paper

Quality Press
600 N. Plankinton Avenue
Milwaukee, Wisconsin 53203
Call toll free 800-248-1946
Fax 414-272-1734
www.asq.org
http://www.asq.org/quality-press
http://standardsgroup.asq.org
E-mail: authors@asq.org

Contents

List of Figures

Introduction

Many new and good ideas are spawned with the asking of a simple question. Such is the genesis of *Six Sigma Marketing* (SSM). Working with a client, a mega dealer of heavy equipment, one of its Black Belts asked, "How do we use Six Sigma to increase market share and revenues?"

It was clear to me that if Six Sigma were to be focused on increasing market share, there had to be some kind of relationship with marketing. After all, in most organizations, market share and revenue growth are the Golden Fleece of marketing. I first talked with a number of Black Belts to get their opinions. Few understood what marketing was all about, and none had any idea of how to focus on market share. They were comfortable with the idea of defects and run times and lower costs, but knew nothing about market share. I then turned to my marketing friends and asked them. They knew little about Six Sigma, and some had no idea that the organization was deploying Six Sigma. To some, Six Sigma was some sort of arcane alchemy that potentially threatened their jobs because of the focus on cost cutting. Thinking that perhaps this was an anomaly, I then turned to other clients but found much the same.

The simple answer seemed to be to apply the principles of Six Sigma to marketing and its constituent components of sales, promotion, product management, pricing, and distribution.

Such is the approach offered by writers such as Michael Pestorius, in *Applying the Science of Six Sigma to the Art of Marketing* (2007). Pestorius applies Six Sigma to such marketing and sales activities as new product sales, sales territory planning, and the promotion process. However, while simply applying Six Sigma, as currently practiced, to marketing might result in less costly marketing activities, this is not the goal. The application of Six Sigma to marketing activities ignores the opportunity to provide a systematic approach for increasing market share. Too many marketing initiatives are based on random efforts. SSM seeks to remove the randomness from marketing and make it more systematic and predictable.

Applying marketing to Six Sigma seemed even less rewarding. Clearly, what was called for was an integration of Six Sigma and marketing, but on what grounds? There needed to be some common elements, such as goals, information needs, tools, and metrics. Accordingly, SSM is defined as:

> a fact-based, data-driven disciplined approach to growing market share by providing targeted product/markets with superior value.

It is organized around the following elements:

- Customer value is the driving strategic metric. It replaces the emphasis on customer satisfaction embraced by both Six Sigma and marketing, and provides a much stronger link to market share gains and revenue increases.

- SSM has a unique set of powerful tools designed around the idea of customer value to concentrate the organization's efforts on both acquisition of new customers and retention of current customers.

- It uses a modified DMAIC (define, measure, analyze, improve, control) model that is not only very familiar to the Six Sigma community but also friendly to and easily understood by marketers.

- It strives to make marketing a more effective and efficient factor within the organization.

- Its goal is defect reduction. A *defect* is defined as failure to provide satisfactory customer events. Customers interact with an organization in many ways: sales, billing inquiries, service, repairs, parts, and so forth. Each event, or interaction, has the ability to increase or decrease their loyalty and hence the organization's market share.

- SSM expands the traditional view of marketing to include emphases not only on pricing, product, promotion, and distribution, but also on processes.

SSM takes elements from both Six Sigma and marketing and forges them into a powerful and focused discipline designed to increase the enterprise's market share and top-line revenues. It is a structured approach that addresses the need for more effective and efficient marketing activities in order to achieve value proposition goals at lower costs. It represents what many have called the next generation in Six Sigma—one not focused solely on reducing costs or defects but actually on increasing revenues and market share.

Marketing has not stayed static since its inception. There have been several different focal areas of marketing, including a commodity approach, an institutional approach, and perhaps most recently a functional approach. Marketing, to maintain its value to an organization, must adapt to the contingencies that surround it. And a major contingency is the emphasis on quality and value. SSM evolved from a frustration with the lack of efficacy of marketing. According to a 2008 survey of the MAPI Marketing Council, "CEOs are growing impatient with marketing. They feel they get accountability for their investments in finance, production, information technology, and even purchasing, but don't know what their marketing spending is achieving." It is time to adapt once again.

On the Six Sigma side, many Black Belts are concerned with a decreasing universe of projects. With a strong concentration on defect reduction and cost cutting, Black Belts are seeking to expand the application of Six Sigma. SSM is a natural byproduct of the frustration with current marketing practices and the longer-term view of many within the Six Sigma community.

As organizations discover the importance of processes and their impact on value delivery, marketing must change from its functional approach and adopt a more process concentration. Value is conveyed to markets in different manners, chief of which is through processes, a perspective that is typically overlooked within a functional environment. Functionalism blinds organizations to processes by creating silos that impede the flow of information and value. SSM represents a breakthrough in this type of thinking and behavior. It becomes the sine qua non of value creation and delivery and competitive performance.

Chapter 1 introduces the reader to the concept of SSM and the rationale for its development and use. Chapter 2 takes on the conventional wisdom regarding customer satisfaction as used in both Six Sigma and marketing, and supplants it with the more powerful and actionable concept of customer value. Chapter 3 provides an overview of the SSM process. A discussion of the DMAIC process with a redefinition of the nature of the define stage is the subject of Chapter 4. Since the focus of SSM is significantly different from its more orthodox counterpart, the definition of its focus will also change. The principal tool used in the define stage is the Product/Market (P/M) Matrix, which augments the more traditional view of market segments. Chapter 5 introduces the reader to the Customer Value Model, the principal tool of the measure stage. The Customer Value Model is the voice of the market (VOM), replacing reliance on the voice of the customer (VOC), and becomes the information platform that launches the rest of the DMAIC process. The analyze stage is the subject of Chapter 6 and is organized around three value tools: the Competitive Value Matrix, the Customer Loyalty Matrix, and the Competitor Vulnerability Matrix. Chapter 7 focuses on yet another tool, the modified Cause and Effect Matrix, which links the organization's performance evaluations on key critical-to-quality factors (CTQs) and attributes to specific value streams and processes. This is the essence of the improve stage. The DMAIC process concludes with Chapter 8 and a discussion of the control stage. Monitoring changes in the organization's competitive value proposition by evaluating customer interactions on critical events is explained. Finally, Chapter 9 offers some discussion on how to implement SSM within the organization.

It is the intention of *Six Sigma Marketing* to challenge the way both the Six Sigma community and the marketing area think about business and the way they currently do business. It does so by providing a detailed and structured approach—one that is entirely data driven—to unleash the power of Six Sigma on the crucial need for revenue growth.

REFERENCE

Pestorius, Michael. 2007. *Applying the Science of Six Sigma to the Art of Marketing.* Milwaukee, WI: ASQ Quality Press.

1

What Is SSM?

A TOO-COMMON SITUATION

I recently accompanied a CEO of a manufactured housing company on a tour of his plant, where he proudly pointed out the changes they had made based on Six Sigma implementations. He talked about the lower cost of production, less rework, quicker fabrication processes, and the overall higher quality of his product. I asked him how these changes had impacted his market share. After a short hesitation he indicated that his share position had not changed that much. I asked him about his customer satisfaction scores. "Not measured," he said.

Shortly thereafter, I had the opportunity to talk with his dealers about the Six Sigma revolution within the organization and its impact on them. The dealers told a completely different story. They did acknowledge a quicker replenishment rate but saw little change in quality. As far as they were concerned, it had nothing to do with them. Furthermore, while production costs at the plant were down, dealer costs were up due to higher costs of setup and repair. I pressed about this. The dealers pointed out that when the product left the plant, it was handled by independent contractors who transported the product to the dealer. Often, product reached its destination with a number of problems incurred during the transportation process: Doors and windows did not align, seams were crooked, electrical hookups were damaged, plumbing was damaged, and so on. The dealer then had to fix these problems and set up the product on the lot for customer inspection. When the home was sold, it was delivered to the customer destination, again by an independent contractor who set up the home on the lot. Not surprisingly, issues with setup were often encountered, causing customer complaints and additional dealer costs. And, as would be expected, not all dealers were responsive to the customer once the product was sold. Many were too focused on making the next sale as opposed to making sure that the customer got the best value.

The lesson to be learned from this is twofold. First, the CEO was too narrowly focused on product. His definition of value was solely product-based and did not conform to how his end user defined value. To the end user, value included not only the product itself but also the delivery, setup, and product support provided by the dealer. In many cases the end user did not differentiate between the manufacturer and the dealer. End users complained about the shoddy production of the manufacturer when in fact many of the problems were the result of a poor setup. In essence, the manufacturer had pushed many of the quality problems he had dealt with or did not deal with at the manufacturing level down the distribution chain.

Second, the CEO fell victim to a false premise: *Value or quality at the point of production does not automatically translate into value or quality at the point of consumption.* This occurs when the organization does not understand how its markets define value and assumes that all value and quality are embedded within the product. It results from a myopic view of value, one often predicated on what the organization thinks is value as opposed to what the customer defines as value. It ignores all other aspects of quality and value that are part of the market's evaluative process.

Can an organization that embraces Six Sigma actually produce the requisite value that drives superior market performance? Can focusing the power of Six Sigma on specific processes within the organization provide a competitive advantage that drives increases in market share? Does quality or value at the point of production automatically translate into value or quality at the point of consumption? Does focusing only on the product actually respond to how end users define value? These are important questions that demand Six Sigma implementations include a focus not only on manufacturing processes but also on how value is actually delivered to the marketplace. This more comprehensive, holistic view must include marketing activities, as they are the essence of SSM.

THE CHALLENGE

Accordingly, one of the most daunting challenges facing the Six Sigma community is how to apply the discipline and methodology of Six Sigma to other organizational activities, in particular the organization's marketing activities. Some have characterized the potential union as a conflict between the disciplined and the undisciplined, the structured and the unstructured, art and science, and so forth. Actually, these characterizations are wrong. There is a natural fit between the two areas and one that promises huge benefits to the organization that can bring this integration about.

Renee Brandon, director of research at Tocquigny, makes a cogent argument and neatly summarizes the issues regarding the inclusion of marketing under a Six Sigma umbrella. She states, rightfully so, that one of the "last areas to be touched by Six Sigma is marketing. . . . And it is one that often inspires either confusion or fear—or both—when mentioned in the context of marketing" (2005, 3).

As further evidence of this lack of integration, consider a recent survey of 951 Six Sigma professionals by *iSixSigma Magazine* (Goeke, Marx, and Reidenbach 2008). When asked to what extent their Six Sigma projects were a direct and explicit outgrowth of their company's competitive marketing strategies, only 13 percent indicated "a great extent." A full 48 percent responded "very little" or "not at all."

One of the major reasons for this lack of integration, according to Brandon, has to do with what she calls the "world of 'defects' and 'control.' This creates one of the reasons that marketing has been slower to adopt Six Sigma than other organizational departments. . . . Six Sigma is about rigorous control to reveal and eliminate unknown variables that can impact a product. However, most marketers know there is no way that they can personally control the many variables that impact their campaigns" (4).

Nonetheless, Brandon argues that "Six Sigma will also need to be adapted to marketing to account for increases in top-line revenue—sales increases, customer acquisition, customer loyalty—rather than being so singularly focused on cost-cutting. Its value should be measured not only by how much it can save a company, but also in how much it can earn a company" (6). It is against this backdrop that the following Six Sigma methodology and approach are offered.

SSM DEFINED

SSM is a fact-based, data-driven disciplined approach to growing market share by providing targeted product/markets with superior value. It accomplishes this enhanced value proposition by:

- Increasing the *effectiveness* and *efficiency* of the organization's value delivery system

- Reducing *customer defects* by focusing on and improving the customer *transaction* or *event* experience

- Using a *modified DMAIC* framework

- Replacing customer satisfaction with customer value as the driving strategic metric

- Employing a set of *unique value tools* not common to most Six Sigma deployments or marketing analyses

- Expanding marketing's functional view to include not only price, product, promotion, and distribution but also *processes*

Increasing the Effectiveness of the Organization's Value Delivery System

For the purpose of SSM, *effectiveness* is defined as achieving or surpassing the market's evaluation of an organization's competitive value proposition. The *competitive value proposition* is your organization's capacity to deliver value relative to that of your competitors and is a strong leading indicator of market share and revenue growth. Every organization typically has multiple value propositions—one for every product/market it chooses to target. A significant mistake is to assume that there is only one—a value proposition for the whole of IBM, or Ford, or FedEx. It is arguably one of the most important assets an organization has under its management because it provides the market with a strong buying signal. It tells buyers the level of value they can expect from an organization's product/service offering relative to what can be expected from competitors' offerings. An important aspect of this value proposition is that if the organization is not actively managing its own value proposition, its competitors are. Because of the relativity of value (one competitor offers greater value than another), failure to manage your value proposition effectively turns it over to your competitors, who are actively managing theirs. It is unlikely that an organization would surrender control of any other asset to the management of its competitors, yet many organizations allow their value proposition to be managed by others. How effective are the organization's quality and marketing efforts at managing this value proposition? Are these efforts measured? Does the organization even consider the value it is providing the market? Does the organization understand what the market means when it talks about value?

Six Sigma advocates often talk about value and its pivotal role in Six Sigma efforts, yet they default to the more conventional customer satisfaction as the goal. Citing that same *iSix-Sigma* survey mentioned earlier (Goeke, Marx, and Reidenbach 2008), when asked "What is the single most important basis for defining the success of your company's Six Sigma initiative?" only 9 percent of these same practitioners responded "increasing customer value," while 18 percent responded with "increasing customer satisfaction." As I will point out in Chapter 2, satisfaction is not the proper metric to use; value is. Accordingly, measuring effectiveness in terms of satisfaction can lead to some serious and erroneous conclusions. Just ask AT&T or Cadillac, whose satisfaction scores were going up while market share was declining!

Increasing the Efficiency of the Organization's Value Delivery System

A second requirement of SSM is the focus on the efficiency with which value reaches the marketplace. This means having the ability to cut all non-value-adding costs, not only in the production of the product or service but also in the delivery and support of the product or service. It means expanding the view of the organization to include its entire value delivery system (including distribution and promotion, not simply the value embedded within the product). It means understanding how the market defines value and then identifying the least cost ways to deliver that value.

In a number of organizations, Six Sigma has been unleashed on processes with an eye to cutting costs. This is fine as long as the costs that are being cut are not involved in creating or delivering value to the end user. Short-term cost gains can be won at the expense of longer-term value problems. The interstices between manufacturing and distribution along the entire supply chain are a source of many non-value-adding costs that impact the organization's efficiency in delivering value to the market.

Reducing Customer Defects by Improving the Customer Transaction Experience

Every time a customer transacts with the organization, it's a test of the organization's competitive value proposition. These transactions or events are like rivets on a plane's wing. Losing one rivet, or even two or three rivets, may not compromise the integrity of the aircraft, but after a certain number of rivets fall off, off comes the wing and down goes the plane. Customers may be willing to suffer through one or more value-reducing transactions, but there will be a limit to what they are willing to tolerate before they take their business to a competitor.

Transactions or events include, but are not necessarily limited to:

- The sales experience

- Customer inquiries (instructions, problem resolution, and so forth)

- Billing inquiries

- Repair

- Customer support (adding account users, adding services, discontinuing services, and so forth)

- Parts purchase

These are the "touch points" customers have with an organization while they are buying a product or service and after they've bought the product or service. Unfortunately, many organizations tend to ignore the customer once the sale is made. Each industry has its own inherent set of transactions necessary for the customer to operate with the organization's product or service. Organizations interact with customers numerous times on a daily basis, all adding up to a large number of potential defect opportunities. How many companies are Six Sigma companies when it comes to customer defects? If the organization is evaluating its performance on these transactions and defines a defect as a score of 7 or below on a 10-point scale, how many defects does it incur over a period of time? How many times does it score a 7 or below? How many know? How many actually measure this? Can you imagine an organization that suffers only 3.4 customer defects per million? Can you imagine the market share of an organization that has achieved a 6σ on customer defects? Can you imagine how difficult it would be to pry a customer from such an organization? At what sigma is your organization operating regarding customer defects? Do you have any idea? Is this important to you? Should it be?

Market share is a function of three factors: acquiring new customers, inducing current customers to purchase more or to purchase more frequently, and retaining current customers. Competition for market share places a huge pressure on customer loyalty, which in turn highly correlates to the organization's capacity to provide defect-free customer transactions. Moreover, transaction evaluations are an important source of information for SSM since they grade the organization's ability to create and deliver value along its entire value delivery system. They can serve as the canary in the mine shaft, alerting management that there is a systematic problem in the value delivery system—one that needs immediate attention and remedy.

Using a Modified DMAIC Approach

SSM does not require reinventing the wheel regarding accepted Six Sigma methodologies. The current and well-accepted DMAIC approach accommodates its specific needs with only slight modifications. While many Six Sigma practitioners might think of the DMAIC process used when an existing product or process is not meeting customer requirements and requires improvement, SSM views the DMAIC process not only in terms of its improvement capacity but also as a basis for *leveraging* a superior performing product or process. When an organization enjoys a value advantage over a targeted competitor, the DMAIC process provides a methodology to take advantage of the superiority, invest in it, and reap the rewards of increased market share accruing to the advantage. This reflects a more strategic view of the DMAIC process and represents a significant point of departure from the more conventional Six Sigma view.

Define

The define stage is where a major difference occurs between traditional Six Sigma and SSM. In the traditional Six Sigma methodology, the define stage is typically focused on clarifying the goals and value of a specific project. It has, as its focus, a predetermined and identified value stream or process. SSM is a market-focused and market-driven methodology. Accordingly, the define stage begins with defining the specific market opportunities for growing the business. These are the specific competitive arenas that the organization is targeting. No project has as of yet been selected since the entire SSM process is informed by the market.

SSM's define stage begins by identifying and prioritizing those product/markets that offer the organization the greatest options for growth. Not all market opportunities are worth investing in. Some will provide high-octane options for economic return, while others become a potential drag and a resource rat hole. Identifying which are which is critical. This means that the opportunities must be evaluated using a quantifiable approach and not one driven by guesses, agendas, or company lore. Quantifying opportunities requires choosing a set of strategic criteria illustrated by the following:

- Market share (current versus potential growth)
- Current size of the market
- Market growth rates
- Competitive intensity
- Lost sales within a product/market
- Margins within the product/market
- Future downstream product support revenues (parts/repairs)
- Synergies with other product/markets

Each product/market is evaluated using this same subset of selected criteria. This ensures a consistent evaluative process that becomes the first step in developing a competitive strategy for the organization.

The conventional Six Sigma define stage begins with identifying the processes that become the focal point of the Six Sigma deployment. This is an internal application of Six Sigma. However, SSM is a market-focused and market-driven approach, and it must first focus on those opportunities that provide the competitive arenas in which the organization chooses to compete for growth. This is a necessary external focus of SSM. At this juncture in the process, there is no information that identifies specific people, product, or processes for value enhancement. It is the market, through the rigorous discipline of SSM, that will identify which people, product, or processes should be targeted for enhanced value delivery. It is the VOM rather than agendas or the internal voices and internal organizational views (read corporate lore or myth) of the marketplace that will dictate which people, products, or processes must be targeted. The P/M Matrix is the principal tool for defining market opportunities for the SS marketer and is the subject of Chapter 4.

Measure

The focus of the measurement phase is to define value for the targeted markets identified in the define stage. The principal tool for this phase is the Competitive Value Model, discussed in great detail in Chapter 5. The Competitive Value Model is the information platform that drives all of SSM. It provides an uninterrupted connection—a flow of information from the targeted markets to subsequent stages of the DMAIC process. For each product/market identified in the define stage, a value model will be generated. Because the definition of value changes from product/market to product/market, so too does the thrust of SSM. It captures the VOM, ensuring that subsequent changes directed by the contingencies of the specific product/market are made.

The value model performs two highly important functions. First, it quantifies the integration between quality and price on the basis of how the market identifies this tradeoff. This eliminates much of the argument about which is more important to the market—quality or price. If price is more important, attention should be directed to finding ways to change the price perception or the actual price. Second, the model identifies and prioritizes the CTQs that drive the value equation and motivate buyers. Without this information, few marketing efforts can satisfy the effectiveness or efficiency criteria so important to SSM efforts.

Analyze

Analysis in the SSM paradigm requires the learning of new tools and their applications. Since SSM is market focused and value driven, these tools are designed to capture and use the market's perception of value. There are three principal tools:

- The Competitive Value Matrix, which depicts the value propositions of your organization and its major competitors

- The Competitive Vulnerability Matrix, which identifies the nature, degree, and strengths and weaknesses of your competitors' value offering

- The Customer Loyalty Matrix, which captures the nature and degree of loyalty of your organization's customer base

These tools provide an analysis of the value landscape within each product/market and provide the basis for identifying how changes in people, product, and processes will enhance the organization's competitive value proposition. All these tools are designed to aid in the growth of market share and top-line revenues. These tools are detailed in Chapter 6.

Improve

Improvement involves mapping targeted processes within specific value streams with the specific objective of improving value disadvantages or enhancing value advantages. Some processes will need improvement in order to close the value gap that exists between your organization and a competitor. This is readily understood. However, for those processes that drive and support a value advantage, enhancement should be the focus. This is called leveraging a strength and often runs opposed to the idea "If it ain't broke, don't fix it!" On the contrary, if it is an advantage, we will want to invest in it to make it even stronger and more powerful. In addition, the improve stage surfaces issues regarding people and products with the same intent—to improve or leverage. The principal tools for the improve stage are a modified Cause and Effect Matrix and Value Stream Mapping. Improvement is the subject of Chapter 7.

Control

Within an SSM world, control focuses on two factors. First, after changes have been made to the value delivery system, SSM requires these changes to be monitored to ensure that they are, in fact, doing what they are supposed to do. Second, the multitude of customer interactions that take place and that represent an early warning system regarding value performance must be tracked and monitored. These control issues are discussed in Chapter 8.

SSM Has Its Own Set of Value-Based Tools

SSM is driven by the premise of providing customers and markets with superior value—the best quality at the most competitive price. Accordingly, the metric that drives SSM is value. SSM is dependent upon several new and unique value tools:

- **The Competitive Value Model.** This model captures the VOM for every targeted product/market in which an organization chooses to compete. The definition of value changes depending upon which market segment is targeted and which product line is the focus. The Competitive Value Model provides two critical pieces of information. First, it clearly identifies the tradeoff between quality and price based on how the market views these two components of value. Which is more important to the market— quality or price? Too often organizations lacking a market focus are pushed into reducing their price, as if this were the only factor that can win market share. This can begin an internecine pricing war that rapidly commoditizes products and services. Understanding which component of value is more important to the market helps avoid this potentially disastrous misstep.

  Second, the value model identifies the CTQs that make up the market's definition of value and prioritizes them in terms of their importance to the market. This eliminates a focus on a relatively unimportant CTQ that has little opportunity for enhancing an organization's competitive value proposition. Using a latent dimension technique can give greater meaning to each of the CTQs. For example, assume the CTQ "responsiveness" emerges. What does responsiveness mean? Ask five Black Belts or marketers to define responsiveness and you will likely get five different answers. Which of these conforms to how the market defines responsiveness? How would you know? The Competitive Value Model defines each CTQ in highly actionable terms that provide direct linkage to key processes and value streams. It directs changes not by internal guessing or agenda but by the VOM.

- **The Competitive Value Matrix.** SSM is all about gaps—value gaps. The Competitive Value Matrix depicts the gaps between competitive products, brands, and services on the basis of two key drivers of value, quality and price, and how the market evaluates each competitive offering. Organizations enjoying a value advantage (a positive value gap) have a clear understanding of how to increase that gap, while those suffering a value disadvantage (a negative value gap) can also use the information to close the value gap. The Competitive Value Matrix provides the first step to competitive strategy based on these gaps. The organization can choose to lead, to challenge, to follow, or to niche.

- **The Competitive Vulnerability Matrix.** On what basis are your competitors vulnerable to competitive intrusion? How do you attack them to acquire new customers? Where are their weak points? This information is detailed in the Competitive Vulnerability Matrix. It is a powerful customer acquisition tool that identifies the low-hanging fruit—those customers who are not getting the value necessary to cement their loyalty to a competitor—and what is the basis of this poor value. This tool provides detailed and actionable information for prying loose those customers at a low cost of acquisition.

- **The Customer Loyalty Matrix.** Market share is a function of three factors: (1) customer acquisition, (2) customer retention, and (3) the increased buying of current customers. How loyal is your customer base? How vulnerable are they to defection? What are the quality or price factors on which your performance is based that are driving them away? Are these factors systemic (based on a sales problem, a distribution problem, a product problem, a process problem, a pricing problem, or a quality problem)? Are there some customers worth saving? This and other types of information are available from the Customer Loyalty Matrix.

SSM Adds a Fifth "P" to the Traditional Four Ps of Marketing

One of the first things that students of marketing are taught is the four Ps—price, product, promotion, and place (distribution). The traditional view of marketing refers to these factors as controllable. According to this approach, value is added by changes and management of these four Ps. SSM adds "process" to this marketing mix. In many cases, value is created and delivered to the market through processes, for example, equipment delivery, repair services, customer service, inquiry handling, billing, and parts sales. SSM forsakes the traditional, functional view of marketing and recognizes the importance of process management and its relationship to overall value creation and delivery. Functionalism creates silos, which are an unintended byproduct of an outdated business approach that fails to understand the dynamic nature and flows of value creation and delivery.

These requirements of SSM form the basis of a methodology that is highly disciplined and highly compatible with the organization that embraces a Six Sigma culture. SSM represents what many refer to as the next horizon or next generation of Six Sigma. It does so not as a competing paradigm but as a synergistic and symbiotic approach to extending Six Sigma ideas, concepts, and methodologies to a heretofore resistant organizational area. SSM turns the power of Six Sigma to external targets, revenue increases, and market share gains.

SSM is an evolving concept. Each enterprise will deploy its own version of SSM based on the principles and tools outlined in this book. SSM represents the integration of a powerful methodology with a critically important function driven by customer definitions of value to bring a disciplined, data-driven, fact-based approach to grow market share and top-line revenues.

REFERENCES

Brandon, Renee. 2005. "The Power of Six Sigma and Marketing: Increased Marketing Effectiveness." Tocquigny white paper, www.tocquigny.com.

Goeke, Reginald, Michael Marx, and Eric Reidenbach. 2008. "Hearing Voices: How Businesses Listen to the Customer." *iSixSigma Magazine*, July/August, 31–38.

2

Value Drives SSM

T he conventional wisdom within the Six Sigma community, as judged by much of the written discourse, is that customer satisfaction is the appropriate strategic measure. For example, in defining Lean Six Sigma, Michael George says the following:

> Lean Six Sigma is a methodology that maximizes shareholder value by achieving the fastest rate of improvement in customer satisfaction, cost, quality, process speed, and invested capital. (2002, 7)

This statement is not compatible with the empirical evidence that exists regarding customer satisfaction and outcome measures such as shareholder value. This chapter challenges the conventional wisdom regarding customer satisfaction, offers evidence of its inappropriateness, and recommends in its place a more powerful and actionable strategic measure—customer value. Customer value is a central component of SSM. It represents more than just the core of the discipline; it is the controllable output of SSM that generates revenues and market share.

SATISFACTION DOES NOT EQUAL VALUE

Most traditional marketing practitioners are perhaps more likely to understand the difference between satisfaction and value. However, it does not appear that this distinction is well understood within the Six Sigma community. For example, Harry and Schroeder discuss customer satisfaction:

> The cycle of detection, analysis and correction ties directly back to the three elements of customer satisfaction—delivering the highest quality product (defect-free products and services), on time (reduced cycle time) and at the right price (which impacts manufacturing costs). (2000, 8)

Forget for the moment the obvious internal manufacturing perspective of this definition, but delivering the highest-quality product at the right cost is the definition of value, not satisfaction. Later on they get it right when they point out:

> Six Sigma is about pursuing quality only if it adds value for the customer and the company. (23)

I point out these issues because there is significant confusion, or at least misunderstanding, regarding the distinction between satisfaction and value. This is more than a simple semantic distinction between satisfaction and value. The distinction has a strong directive implication not only for Six Sigma but more importantly for SSM.

A DISTINCTION OF IMPORTANCE

The concept of value is at least as old as this country. Adam Smith talked about value in his monumental work, *The Wealth of Nations*, published in 1776. What is new about value is our ability to measure it, and with the power of measurement comes an even greater ability to manage it. Value is a powerful force in a competitive free market system—the sine qua non of our exchange process. For any kind of exchange to take place, the buyer must value what the seller offers, and the seller, in turn, must value what the buyer has to offer. This is a simple but powerful concept that drives a free or relatively free market system.

Value is an inextricable shaper of companies, markets, and industries. One only has to look at the history of the U.S. auto industry, where Japanese quality provided at a good price caused U.S. automakers to hemorrhage market share until the Big Three no longer included Chrysler but Toyota and, in the future, those who can get the value equation right (see Figure 2.1).

Similarly, the battle for retail supremacy between Kmart and Wal-Mart was decided on the value battlefield, with Wal-Mart emerging as the clear victor. Organizations that fall into the "value pit" face a very hard climb out. Some never make it.

The U.S. market

The big five
Share of the total U.S. market for each month.
Below, 12-month rolling averages from Nov. 1998 through Nov. 2008.

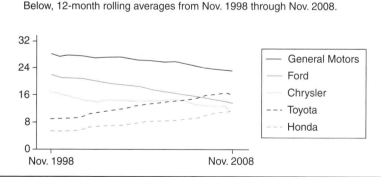

Figure 2.1 Eroding market share of automakers.
Source: *Wall Street Journal* Online.

VALUE VERSUS SATISFACTION

The proper place to start understanding value and satisfaction, and the distinction between the two, is by defining the two concepts. *Value* is the relationship between the quality of a product or service and the price the customer pays to obtain that product or service. A clear but simple example involves the comparison of value for a beer lover. Which beer offers the greater value: a high-quality beer costing $1 or a beer of similar quality costing $2? Most beer aficionados would opt for the first beer. This brings us to the first proposition regarding value: It involves a cognitive calculation of the interaction between quality and price. It is a thinking decision—one that requires an evaluation.

Value Hinges on Quality

It also makes clear that if value is to be managed, we had better understand how the market defines quality. This is where much of the problem resides.

Quality to the end user is more than simple *product* quality. Focus group after focus group of customers talking about value and quality across a multitude of industries proves this point. Quality is defined and impacted by the entire value creation and delivery system. It includes evaluations of how the product was sold, delivered, serviced, billed, and supported. In fact, in many manufacturing situations, customers talk about the importance of the dealer and dealer services as being significantly more important than the product itself! Figure 2.2 offers a comprehensive perspective of how end users define value and quality.

Many U.S. organizations continue to define quality solely from the myopic perspective of product. Figure 2.2 is a generalized depiction of quality and value developed from a large number of focus groups. And, as the figure points out, it is significantly more complex than a simple product definition of quality. The flip side of the complexity is the completeness of the

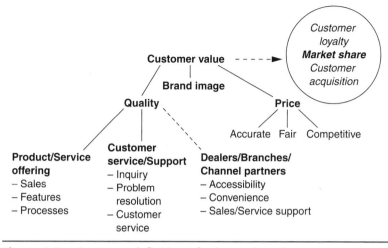

Figure 2.2 Customer definition of value and quality.

generic definition and the actionable guidelines that it provides. It is directive in nature and not only speaks to your customers but outlines the factors that drive the market's definition of quality.

Quality is a multidimensional factor. It contains the product component, but equally important, it contains a customer service/support component and a dealer channel element. Consider how customers typically evaluate an automobile purchase. They may start with a make and nameplate. Then the decision often turns to the dealer. Which dealer can provide the best hassle-free service and the best price? Given that many automobiles are not distinguished by a quality difference, the dealer becomes a critical factor.

Several years ago while working on a project with Caterpillar, I had the opportunity to talk with a young CAT engineer who was working in a specific product group. This engineer admitted that CAT no longer had a significant product quality or technological advantage over its competition. The product quality gap had narrowed significantly. The engineer said, "We can no longer create the quality and value advantage in the manufacturing process. We can provide sufficient quality to keep us in the game but it's the dealer who wins us the business. It is at the dealer level where much of the value is created." Some CAT executives may or may not agree with this assessment, but working with a large number of heavy-equipment manufacturers over time, one thing has emerged: The most important CTQs, as defined by the buyer, are those associated with the dealer. It is, in fact, the dealer that creates the major portion of value for its targeted markets. Quality and value transcend a simple product focus and encompass aspects of the entire value delivery system.

The challenge facing the quality community is to understand how its targeted markets define quality and what the calculation is that these markets use in evaluating the value of the different competitive offerings they can choose from. What is the tradeoff between quality and price? How does the market prioritize the CTQs—which are most important and which are least important? This evaluation process is a *cognitive* process—a *thinking* process.

Satisfaction, on the other hand, is an emotional response to a purchase. The customer *feels* satisfied; the customer doesn't *think* satisfied. Satisfaction equates to happiness. If we are satisfied with our purchase experience, we are happy. This was reflected in a recent ASQ customer satisfaction workshop entitled "Keep Your Current Customers Happy."

Going back to our simple beer example, we can make the following statements about value and satisfaction. Once we have paid for and consumed the beer, we can determine whether we were happy with our purchase and experience. This is a *reactive* response. Value, on the other hand, is a *proactive* response. Six Sigma marketers can determine what beer drinkers value in a beer—its taste elements, its packaging, its availability, its image, and of course, the price they are willing to pay for all the different quality components. They can determine the relative importance of these quality components leading to the creation and delivery of a beer with a dominating value proposition, responsive to a targeted product/market.

Too often the concepts of satisfaction and value are used as if they were synonyms. This is incorrect since they represent two distinct dynamics associated with the buying decision. *We buy on value and repurchase based on the satisfaction of the value we received.* Again, value is a proactive metric—one that informs decisions regarding the traditional marketing mix (price, product, promotion, and distribution)—while satisfaction is a reaction in response to our value proposition. In this, value is a strategic measure, while satisfaction is a transactional measure best used in post-purchase situations to evaluate how responsive the enterprise is to the market's definition of value.

HAPPY CUSTOMERS ARE NOT ALWAYS PROFITABLE OR LOYAL CUSTOMERS

Consider how the ACSI (American Customer Satisfaction Index) is calculated. It involves the difference between what the customer expects in the transaction and what the customer actually receives (air flight, dining experience, and so forth). Is the expectation about a specific attribute or CTQ, or is it about some other more global measure? The expectation is about value (the relationship of quality to price), which is then compared with the actual value the customer receives. The difference, if positive, is satisfaction—the actual experience is greater than what was expected. Conversely, if the actuality of the transaction is less than the expectation, a state of dissatisfaction exists. Satisfaction is a transaction-based measure about value where the value proposition of the product or service in the transaction has been strategically formulated.

We want the strategic measure to be predictive of some desired outcome, such as increases in top-line revenues or market share. From the traditional Six Sigma perspective, we seek an $X \rightarrow Y$ relationship. Value is the measure that does this, not satisfaction. Satisfaction has little, if any, predictive capabilities. Consider the evidence offered in Figure 2.3.

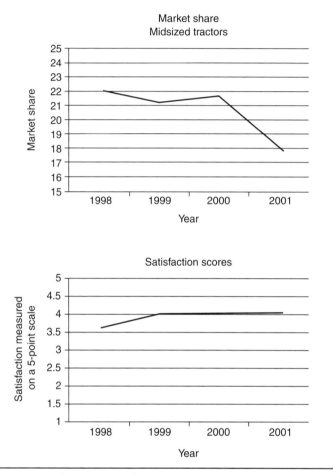

Figure 2.3   Market share and customer satisfaction.

The top graph shows the actual market share changes facing this manufacturing company, while the bottom graph depicts the changes in customer satisfaction (on a five-point scale) for this same company over the same time period. Clearly, the company is losing market share in the face of increasing customer satisfaction scores. Does satisfaction predict market share? Are satisfied customers loyal customers? The answer is a resounding no!

Frederick Reichheld points out the lack of relationship between satisfaction and organizational performance:

> Most customer satisfaction surveys aren't very useful. They tend to be long and complicated, yielding low response rates and ambiguous implications that are difficult for operating managers to act on. Furthermore, they are rarely challenged or audited because most senior executives, board members and investors don't take them seriously. *That's because their results don't correlate tightly with profits or growth.* (2003, 2–3; emphasis added)

Reichheld continues:

> Our research indicates that satisfaction lacks a consistently demonstrable connection to actual customer behavior and growth. This finding is born out by the short shrift that investors give to such reports as the American Consumer Satisfaction Index. The ACSI, published quarterly in the *Wall Street Journal*, reflects the customer satisfaction ratings of some 200 U.S. companies. In general it is difficult to discern a strong correlation between high customer satisfaction scores and outstanding sales growth. Indeed in some cases, there is an inverse relationship; at Kmart, for example, a significant increase in the company's ACSI was accompanied by a sharp decrease in sales as it slid into bankruptcy. (4)

Reichheld concludes with one other piece of proof—this one from the auto industry:

> The marketing executive at the company wanted to understand why, after the firm had spent millions of dollars on customer satisfaction surveys, satisfaction ratings for individual dealers did not relate very closely to dealer profits or growth. (4)

In my own consulting work with different types of organizations, the lack of relationship between satisfaction and performance is well understood. Banks with high ROAs (return on assets) sometimes have the lowest satisfaction scores. Companies with high satisfaction scores are losing market share. During one seminar with a group of marketing analysts, I challenged participants to offer evidence that satisfaction has a relationship with market or financial performance measures. Only one person spoke up. She said that her organization had done extensive analytical work on satisfaction and found that an R^2 of .25 existed between satisfaction and sales. I pointed out that the R^2 statistic indicated the amount of variance explained in the dependent variable (sales) by the independent variable (satisfaction). Translating this into English means that satisfaction explains only 25 percent of the changes in sales. Put another way, 75 percent of the changes in sales were explained by some other factor or factors. Not convincing testimony to the power of satisfaction. This strongly suggests that by attempting to improve satisfaction, you will get only marginal returns to sales, if any at all.

No wonder traditional marketing has come under such withering criticism as a cost as opposed to a revenue generator. Yvonne Tocquigny (2005), CEO of Tocquigny, points out the failure of traditional marketing practices:

> It is not unusual today to see marketing investments that produces (sic) a negative return on investments (ROI), or have a success rate that is close to zero. According to the June 2005 issue of *Harvard Business Review*, citing data from Copernicus Marketing Consulting:
>
> - 84% of programs are second rate, leading to a decline in brand equity and market share
>
> - 4% is as good as it gets for advertising ROI
>
> - 74% is the less-than-stellar figure for customer satisfaction.

She continues:

> Other measures are consistent with these findings. The
> Marketing Measurement Association, for example, reports
> only a $58 return on every $100 invested in marketing. The
> Marketing Science Institute reports that a 100% increase
> in marketing expenditures yields just a 1% increase in
> sales. . . . In this new environment of accountability, they
> (traditional marketers) must prove marketing operations
> represent a value center rather than a cost center.

Value—customer value, that is—is a strong leading indicator
of growth and profitability. Here's some proof from Brad Gale,
author of the 1994 book *Managing Customer Value*:

> AT&T spent the years after its breakup in 1983 losing
> market share. . . . The losses were particularly painful to
> quality advocates, because AT&T's old fashioned "cus-
> tomer satisfaction" surveys showed the company scor-
> ing well even in the businesses that were losing share
> most dramatically. In long distance, the company's core
> business, the share losses were running at six points a
> year—equivalent to more than a billion dollars a year in
> sales. (6)

Gale quantifies the degree to which value (market-perceived
quality) impacts earnings:

> Using the market-perceived quality metric (value) . . . and
> the Profit Impact of Market Strategy (PIMS) database,
> we can demonstrate that the companies who move into a
> superior quality (value) position with a market-perceived
> quality ratio that is at least 24% better than their competi-
> tors earn a return-on-sales of more than 12 percent. . . .
> Businesses that get pushed into an inferior quality posi-
> tion with a market-perceived quality ratio that is 24% or

more worse than the competition earn a profit that is less than 4% of sales. (15–16)

Gale concludes:

> Superior customer value is the best leading indicator of market share and competitiveness. And market share and competitiveness in turn drive the achievement of long term financial goals such as profitability, growth, and shareholder value. (26)

It would appear that Michael George's definition cited in the beginning of this chapter is somewhat flawed, as he tries to relate shareholder value to improvements in customer satisfaction. There is little, if any, empirical proof regarding this relationship. It is based on the faulty notion that a happy customer is a profitable customer. I call this the "contented customer theory" of traditional marketing. SSM jettisons this outdated thinking and embraces the more empirical and fact-based relationship between performance outcomes and customer value.

ONE FINAL WORD

The foregoing gives some additional insight into how the two metrics should be used. Satisfaction is a good report card measure of how an organization has handled a transaction. If a person takes a car into a repair shop and pays for repair services, gauging the customer's satisfaction tells us whether the customer is happy with the repair work. If the customer is unhappy, we might want to find out why, especially if there is a systematic pattern to the unhappiness across customers. If the customer is happy, the likelihood of that customer returning is increased—at least until the customer finds the same level of happiness at a lower price or better value elsewhere. Value tells us how important the repair function is within the entire ownership experience and how to manage it to produce a satisfied customer. Issues of on-time delivery, cleanliness, parts availability, knowledgeable technicians, clean waiting rooms, easy-to-understand invoices, and courtesy all combine to define the repair process, and in so doing tell us how to manage it a priori. The satisfaction score is our ex post facto value grade.

Value is also a metric that applies to all products or services within a specific market. Take, for instance, automobiles. Within a specific class of automobiles, customers in a targeted segment use a common calculus to determine which nameplates offer the best value. Satisfaction can vary from customer to customer, but within a specific market segment a general value definition can be determined. Satisfaction is affected by the delivery of that value and may be impacted by any aspect of the transaction. That is why value is best measured across a market where satisfaction is a customer-specific measure.

Would you expect buyers in your targeted markets to buy from you if they saw little value in doing so? Would you buy a product or do business with a company that provided you with little value? Would you continue to pay a high price for low-quality products or services? Are you any different from your customers, both actual and potential? The answers are no, no, no, and no.

Another final word, and also a personal observation. It amazes me how many organizations have embraced the idea of a dashboard to help manage their business. For those organizations that are even somewhat market focused, it's not uncommon to see a satisfaction box or two on the dashboard along with the requisite performance metrics: revenues, market share, unit sales, profits, and so forth—lagging indicators all! Why would you construct a backward-looking dashboard? Is it because you wanted to understand why you lost sales, market share, and revenues after they were lost? Why wouldn't you want a forward-looking dashboard that could tell you about revenues, market share, sales, and so forth, before you suffered losses? Why wouldn't you want a leading indicator of performance that could act as the canary in the mine shaft? Customer satisfaction is a backward-looking metric—a hallmark of a failing traditional marketing function. Customer value is a forward-looking, predictive metric that is the core of SSM.

It is no small thing to change entrenched ideas. The conventional wisdom yields grudgingly and haltingly. More and more organizations, however, are challenging the "contented customer theory of marketing" and turning to customer value. Customer value, because of its relationship to market share and revenue growth, is a foundational concept of SSM as well as the strategic metric that drives a fact-based, data-driven methodology.

REFERENCES

Gale, Bradley T. 1994. *Managing Customer Value: Creating Quality and Service That Customers Can See*. New York: The Free Press.

George, Michael. 2002. *Lean Six Sigma: Combining Six Sigma Quality with Lean Speed*. New York: McGraw-Hill.

Harry, Mikel, and Richard Schroeder. 2000. *Six Sigma: The Breakthrough Management Strategy Revolutionizing the World's Top Corporations*. New York: Currency.

Reichheld, Frederick. 2003. "The One Number You Need to Grow." *Harvard Business Review*, December, 1–11.

Tocquigny, Yvonne. 2005. "The Quest for Quality: Applying Six Sigma Principles to Marketing." Tocquigny white paper, www.tocquigny.com.

3

Integrating Six Sigma and Marketing with the Competitive Planning Process

The integrating activity that brings Six Sigma and marketing together and launches SSM on targeted value opportunities is the competitive planning process. It provides a logical, step-by-step process that gives SSM a laserlike focus on markets, market share, and revenue growth. The integration of the planning process with the structure of the DMAIC process provides a data-driven approach for removing the guesswork and agendas that often drive traditional marketing activities. The integration of the competitive planning process and the DMAIC approach to produce the architecture for SSM is shown in Figure 3.1.

SSM provides a structured approach to problem solving and addresses the problem of how to grow market share. To understand how this works, a brief discussion of planning is in order.

PLANNING HIERARCHIES

There are typically three levels of planning within organizations: a corporate level, a strategic business unit (SBU) or

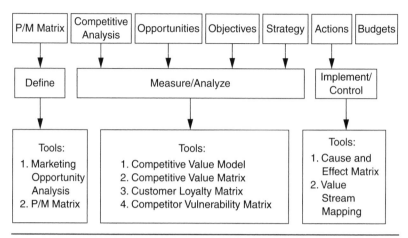

Figure 3.1   The integration of Six Sigma and marketing.

division level, and a product/market level. Each has different purposes. Figure 3.2 shows this planning hierarchy.

Corporate Level Planning

Corporate level planning is designed to answer the question, "How does the organization grow?" It is a high-level plan that directs the other two levels of planning. Essentially there are four options at this level:

- Market penetration—Selling more of the organization's current product lines to its currently targeted markets

- Product development—Developing new products to sell to its current markets

- Market development—Selling current products to new markets

- Diversification—Selling new products to new markets

The organization, in choosing how to grow, will often utilize several of these options.

Figure 3.2　Planning hierarchy.

SBU Level Planning

SBUs are separate divisions within an organization. Typically each SBU:

- Has its own business mission
- Is made up of related products and markets
- Has its own set of competitors
- Has its own manager
- Can be planned independent of other business units

The task of SBU planning is to answer the question, "Where does the organization choose to compete?" This is where the P/M Matrix (discussed in Chapter 4) becomes an important tool in initiating the modified DMAIC process. Since not all growth opportunities are the same for the SBU, it is necessary to identify the different opportunities, evaluate them by using strategic criteria, and then prioritize them for action.

Product/Market Level Planning

Competitive planning takes place at the product/market level. For each product/market selected, there must be a competitive plan developed. The overriding question to be answered at this level of planning is, "How does the organization compete?" Each product/market will have different definitions of value, different sets of competitors, and different competitive dynamics, all of which necessitate different competitive plans. It is at this level that SSM plays a critically important role.

SSM cannot effectively be deployed at the corporate level or at the SBU level. These levels are too far removed from the competitive arena where SSM has its application. At these higher levels, there is inadequate specific market information regarding performance of people, product, or processes. Global information does exist, but it lacks the granularity to drive change in the organization's competitive value proposition at the specific market level. The objective of SSM is on the growth of market share by value enhancement. The necessary questions regarding both market share and value enhancement cannot be answered at the higher levels of planning, rendering SSM ineffective at those levels. It is only once the specific product/markets have been targeted that SSM can be deployed.

THE COMPETITIVE PLANNING PROCESS

Figure 3.3 identifies the steps in the competitive planning process, beginning with the P/M Matrix. This is the principal tool used in the define stage of SSM.

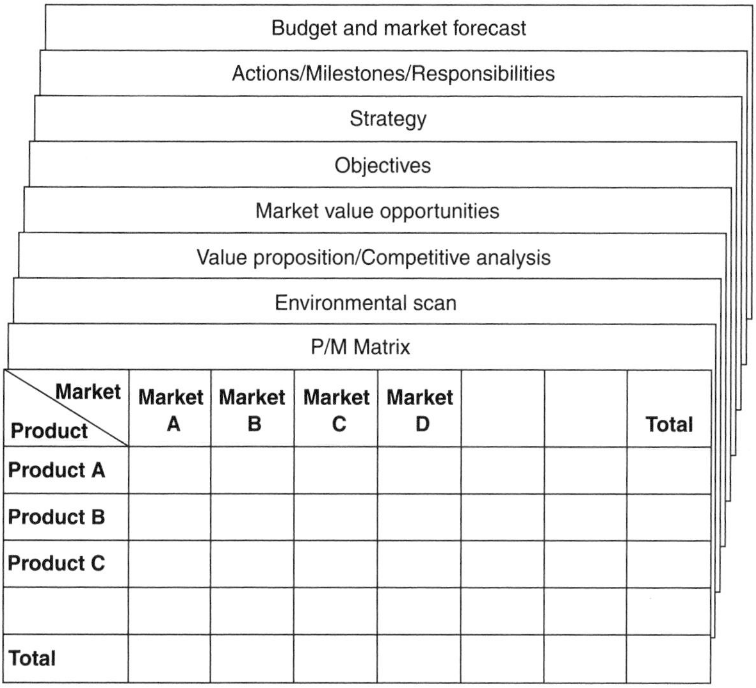

Market Product	Market A	Market B	Market C	Market D			Total
Product A							
Product B							
Product C							
Total							

Figure 3.3 The competitive planning process.

The Value Proposition/Analysis Step

The value proposition/analysis step corresponds to the measure and analysis steps in the SSM process. Here the principal tools are:

- The Competitive Value Model, which identifies the tradeoff between quality and price and identifies and ranks the CTQs. This is discussed in Chapter 5.

- The Competitive Value Matrix, the Competitive Vulnerability Matrix, the Customer Loyalty Matrix, and the Cause and Effect Matrix. These tools are the subjects of Chapters 6 and 7.

Identifying Market Value Opportunities

Identifying market value opportunities is a unique part of SSM. SSM focuses on the market and specifically on the value proposition of the organization operating within that market. Market value opportunities are generated from the information regarding competitive advantages and disadvantages. The focus of this step is to identify specific opportunities to either narrow or widen the gap between your organization and a competitor, and in doing so, to change market share in a positive direction.

Figure 3.4 provides an approach for identifying and prioritizing the different value opportunities.

The vertical side of the matrix lists the three possible outcomes from a comparison of strengths and weaknesses. The organization can have a strength, be at parity, or have a weakness to the targeted competitor. Across the top are two types

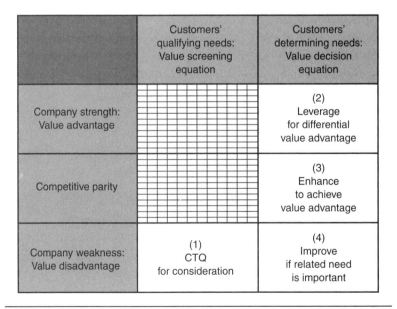

	Customers' qualifying needs: Value screening equation	Customers' determining needs: Value decision equation
Company strength: Value advantage		(2) Leverage for differential value advantage
Competitive parity		(3) Enhance to achieve value advantage
Company weakness: Value disadvantage	(1) CTQ for consideration	(4) Improve if related need is important

Figure 3.4   Prioritizing value opportunities.

of needs: a qualifying need and a determining need. *Qualifying needs*, which go by names such as "table stakes" or "must-haves," are the needs that have to be satisfied in order to be considered as part of the buyer's evoked set. An example will explain this. If price is a qualifier, the buyer will consider only those options that fall within an acceptable price range. If an organization falls outside this range (on the upward side), it will not qualify and will not be considered. Here's another example. A heavy-equipment dealer could not sell trucks in a certain area of a region because the dealer could not meet the noise abatement regulations of that region. Again, it could not qualify and accordingly was not considered when it came time to buy trucks. Once the organization becomes qualified (falls into the price range or meets noise abatement levels), there is no need to spend resources trying to improve. You either qualify or do not qualify. It makes no sense to invest further.

If qualifiers get you into the game, determiners will win the game. The organization's performance on a determiner is the differentiator that makes the organization and its products or services a compelling buying option. These are the CTQs that lead to a differential value advantage.

The first place to consider a value opportunity is in regard to qualifiers and the organization's weakness on them. The P/M Matrix permits the organization to identify key growth options. Each product/market will have its own set of qualifiers. If a product/market is targeted, it is because of its economic value to the organization. Consequently, qualification is the first order of business. Failure to qualify either bars entry to this market or, at best, retards penetration.

The second place to look for value opportunities is in the organization's strength or advantage on a key determining need (CTQ). It is tempting to focus on a weakness that the organization has on a CTQ, but the organization can achieve greater returns by leveraging a strength. By doing so, the organization can expect a greater change in its competitive value proposition and a greater return on its objective of share increase.

Third, look to those areas where the organization is at parity on a CTQ or determining need. Parity says that your performance is equal to that of the targeted competitor. By investing in this CTQ to enhance your performance, you achieve a degree of competitive separation from the targeted competitor and now enjoy an advantage or strength that can be further leveraged.

Finally, invest in those CTQs that are weaknesses or disadvantages, especially if they are important. The value model will tell you this. If they are not important, they may not warrant further investment. That, of course, will depend on the specific dynamics of the product/market.

For example, assume that organization XYZ has no weakness on a qualifier but does have a weakness to a targeted competitor on an important CTQ called "customer focus." It has no strengths to leverage. Its first opportunity is clear—to improve customer focus. This same approach would be used to specify the opportunity to improve XYZ's performance on other CTQs for which it has a disadvantage. If it was at parity regarding other CTQ performance with the targeted competitor, these opportunities would follow in priority.

Performance Objectives

There are two kinds of major performance objectives in SSM— business objectives and value objectives. Business objectives are articulated for each targeted product/market and address two key areas—market share and value.

Business Objectives

Business performance objectives include market share, margins, revenues, unit sales, or some combination of these. SSM typically focuses on market share, revenues, or unit sales without a reduction in margins. A component of the objective is the time horizon, which in most cases will encompass one year at a time and up to three years overall. This allows the tracking of progress toward the goal over time.

Business performance objectives should, of course, conform to the basic requirements of all good objectives—specific, reachable, time bound, and quantifiable (capable of being measured). Here are some objectives from a planning team who was developing a competitive plan for their business:

> *P/M objectives:* Increase market share from 18 percent in 2006 to 19 percent by year-end 2007, to 21 percent by year-end 2008, to 23 percent by year-end 2009.

The objective is specific, reachable, time bound, and quantifiable.

Value Objectives

Value objectives relate to the organization's competitive value proposition. As a leading indicator of market share, the organization's competitive value performance must have its own set of objectives. The information driving the setting of these objectives comes from the main SSM tools discussed in subsequent chapters. Here is the corresponding set of value objectives for the same firm:

> *Value objectives:* Increase score on customer partnering CTQ from 7.98 to 8.87 by year-end 2006, to 9.00 by year-end 2007, and to 9.20 by year-end 2008. Achieve customer retention rates of 85 percent or higher during this same time period.

Again, the objective is specific, reachable, time bound, and quantifiable.

Crafting Strategies

Crafting strategies is a lot easier than is often portrayed, especially within the paradigm of SSM. Strategies emanate from a data-driven approach, not plucked out of thin air. There are four basic options:

- To lead
- To challenge
- To follow
- To niche

Leadership is possible when the organization has an advantage on one or more CTQs. Investing in these CTQs to increase the gap leads to even greater leadership position, with corresponding increases in market share. Too many companies finding an advantage on a CTQ are content to slap themselves on the back and not invest further to use this CTQ to dominate competitors. Over time, this advantage can be eroded and leadership can be lost. Lead from strength is a premise of SSM.

Challengers are those organizations that have either a small disadvantage or a parity position with targeted competitors. Here the strategy is to invest in CTQ improvement to close the gap and eventually overtake the targeted competitor. This may take some time since improvements may not immediately show up in the marketplace.

Followers are those organizations that have a disadvantage and lack the resources to significantly close the gap. Their strategy is not to lose ground to the targeted competitor. It may be that the organization does not have the financial resources available at this time to challenge but will have them at a later time. By following, the organization is dependent on share increases through the organic growth of the product/market and not the efforts of the following organization.

Finally, *nichers* are those organizations that do not have the necessary product or service depth or breadth to compete across the board. They may be companies with limited distribution and can only compete effectively in specific regions. By niching, their strategy is to specialize and penetrate the product/market on their own limiting terms.

Coupling the strategy position (lead, challenge, follow, or niche) with the specific value opportunities completes the strategy to become the undisputed value leader by:

- Improving awareness of our product offering and associated services, and improving sales coverage (*qualifier*)

- Improving to leverage our dealer service

- Improving to leverage our brand's strong and recognized machine quality and brand image by emphasizing key features

- Improving to leverage our partnering capabilities by focusing on our high-quality sales personnel

- Improving to leverage our parts supply performance

The strategy reflects several aspects of the SSM process. First, the company is choosing to be a leader—note the terminology "undisputed leader." This is because the company was sharing a leadership position (at parity) with its main competitor. Second, there is a weakness on a qualifier (awareness) that was impeding its penetration into targeted product/markets. Third, the parity position is reflected in the opportunities—to improve to leverage. Improving on these CTQs allows the company to ultimately leverage its improvements as strengths.

Strategy in SSM is a structured, disciplined, and data-driven process. It is not based on agendas or chimeras that materialize out of thin air. SSM strategies use the VOM to generate and articulate courses of action that are focused on value enhancement and market share gains—the twin objectives of SSM.

Marketing Mix Objectives

Each value opportunity will require a unique set of marketing mix objectives to ensure its accomplishment. The marketing mix for traditional marketing organizations includes what are known as the four Ps—product, price, promotion, and place (distribution). In SSM a fifth "P" is added—process. These are the controllable variables of the organization. They are the vehicles that drive changes in the organization's competitive value proposition and market share.

Here is an example of a firm that sells forklifts. Its strategy, which was shown earlier, is to become the undisputed value leader by:

- Improving awareness of our product offering and associated services, and improving sales coverage

- Improving to leverage our dealer service

- Improving to leverage our brand's strong and recognized machine quality and brand image by emphasizing key features

- Improving to leverage our partnering capabilities by focusing on our high-quality sales personnel

- Improving to leverage our parts supply performance

This company was at parity on value with its targeted competitor. It was not differentiated in the eyes of the market, and there was no single value leader.

The first opportunity is a qualifier. The company was not enjoying the visibility and awareness necessary to be involved in many choice decisions. In those cases where it was seeking to "improve to leverage," it was at parity with its major competitor on those specific CTQs.

Figure 3.5 illustrates how the company developed its marketing mix objectives for the first four opportunities.

Objectives
Opportunity #1: Improving awareness of our product and associated services, and improving sales coverage

Promotion

1.1 Attain 70% unaided awareness of XYZ as a supplier of lift trucks by end of 2006

1.2 Attain 85% unaided awareness of XYZ as a supplier of lift trucks by end of 2007

1.3 Attain 95% unaided awareness of XYZ as a supplier of lift trucks by end of 2008

1.4 50% of all Warehousing customers likely to buy 1 or more lift trucks within 1 year will receive a face-to-face sales call once/quarter

1.5 XYZ in on 55% of all lift truck deals by end of 2008

Opportunity #2: Improving to leverage XYZ's dealer service

Process

2.1 95% of all shop and field service work completed on time as promised

2.2 Major repair (e.g., drive train) completion times reduced by 25% from current levels

2.3 95% of all breakdown problems correctly diagnosed in the field within 2 hours of arrival on site (same criterion in shop for equipment delivered by customer)

Place (Distribution)

2.4 All emergency breakdowns (metro areas) responded to on-site within 2 hours

2.5 80% on-site 4–6 hours in non-metro areas (within 75 miles of branch)

Promotion/Communication

2.6 For every repair situation (outside field), customer notified of repair status every 24 hours

Opportunity #3: Improving to leverage [brand name]'s strong and recognized machine quality and brand image by emphasizing key features

Product

3.1 All new machine deliveries accompanied by DVD on safe and effective operation

3.2 All machine deliveries to customers who have not previously owned a [brand name] lift truck accompanied by 1 hour live operations demonstration

Figure 3.5 Marketing mix objectives.

Following are features that should be demonstrably superior:

Larger drive motors compared to all other competitors
Speed
Turning radius
Smooth braking

Promotion
3.3 50% of LT/Warehousing market rate [brand name] lift trucks as providing superior operator comfort, durability, ease of on/off, and ease of operation relative to [Competitor 3] and all other major players
3.4 50% of LT/Warehousing market rate [brand name] accessibility of work areas for scheduled servicing as being superior

Opportunity #4: Improving to leverage XYZ's dealer partnering by focusing on our high-quality sales personnel

Product
4.1 All sales reps capable of operating a lift truck to level 1 of operator competency
4.2 Sales reps capable of explaining functionality of every aspect of [brand name] and key competitive lift trucks
4.3 Sales reps demonstrate working knowledge of accounting, tax, depreciation, and financial operations of the client's business pertinent to Warehousing customers
4.4 All Warehousing reps understand current and prospective projects in the region

Promotion
4.5 All Warehousing reps understand and able to deliver the company's core values (pertains to ethics, integrity, honesty, excellence in all things)
4.6 80% of Warehousing market aware of XYZ commitment to Warehousing market with [location] facility and dedicated personnel

Figure 3.5 Marketing mix objectives. (Continued)

Its first opportunity was improving awareness and sales coverage. This is a qualifier. Without the requisite awareness and coverage, it was not being considered as part of the buying set. And since this was primarily a promotion problem, the promotion element played a significant role. The promotion objectives are clear, quantifiable, reachable, and time bound, as all good objectives should be.

Its second opportunity—to improve to leverage XYZ's dealer service—involved three mix components: a process component, a distribution component, and a promotion component. The process component had three objectives:

- 95 percent of all shop and field service work completed on time as promised

- Major repair (for example, drive train) completion times reduced by 25 percent from current levels

- 95 percent of all breakdown problems correctly diagnosed in the field within two hours of arrival on site

Clearly, improving shop and field services and major repair service requires improving the repair *process*. Repair or service is not a function but rather a series of processes that begin with and include the following:

- Customer inquiry

- Credit checking

- Scheduling

- Transportation

- Diagnosis

- Parts delivery

- Repair

- Delivery

- Billing

Similarly, the correct diagnosis of breakdowns is also process dependent. The diagnosis process might include these subprocesses:

- Inspection

- Stripping

- Cleaning

- Diagnosing

The distribution objective similarly involves the response process with all of its component subprocesses.

To accomplish these objectives it was necessary to map the different value streams and to identify what impediments might exist in achieving the stated objectives. The remaining opportunities demonstrate the nature of marketing mix objectives and how they relate to the specific opportunities.

Actions/Milestones/Responsibilities

The actions/milestones/responsibilities portion of the competitive plan detail the what, when, and who of plan implementation. It is in this portion of the competitive planning process that the improve and control aspects of the DMAIC model are brought into play. For each mix objective there will be a set of steps or actions to accomplish the objective, a timetable as to when each action will be accomplished, and an individual who is responsible for each action. Examples are shown in Figure 3.6.

It is at this point in the action list that SSM actually focuses on how to improve value delivery. For example, referring back to Opportunity 2 (to improve to leverage XYZ's dealer service), it was obvious that an analysis of the dealer service value stream was necessary. This conclusion resulted from the structured approach of SSM that analyzes the dealer value stream, implements changes, and sets up controls to ensure that the changes made in the value stream show up in the marketplace as positive changes in the organization's competitive value proposition.

Once actions have been identified, milestones are attached. This ensures that the plan is kept on track and provides checkpoints for plan monitoring. By assigning responsibilities to each action, accountability is provided.

Action	Key milestone	Performance measure	Responsibility	Cost
Assess performance gaps on CTQ factors relative to Competitor 3	April 2005	Performance gaps quantified and rank ordered according to their importance	John Schimmel	-0-
Identify performance gaps relative to Competitor 3 for each performance attribute within the most important CTQ factor	April 2005	Importance weights established for each performance attribute	John Schimmel	-0-
Flesh out Y platform to confirm value stream for analysis	May 2005	Y = #1 CTQ; Sub-Ys = Performance attributes with importance weights Identification of input processes (Xs) affecting the outputs (Ys)	Jim Plummer	-0-
Develop and evaluate CTQ/ Process Matrix	May 2005	Impact of processes on attributes assessed and weights assigned. Processes ranked in terms of impact on quality driver attributes and cost.	Jim Plummer	-0-
Develop map of value stream	May 2005	Skeletal map of complete value stream with swim lanes. Detailed map of priority processes. Problem areas identified.	Roger Lauck	-0-

Figure 3.6　Actions for Objective 2.1 (95 percent of all shop and field service work completed on time as promised).

Select/define Lean Six Sigma projects	June 2005	Impact of identified problems on quality driver and on cost assessed. Opportunities and objectives identified. Rank order based on impact. Top 3 opportunities selected. Approval by Lean Six Sigma sponsor.	Peter Hall	-0-
Determine baseline performance criteria	July 2005	% of work orders with promise dates included. % of completes within promise date. % defects, etc.	John Schimmel	-0-

Figure 3.6   Actions for Objective 2.1 (95 percent of all shop and field service work completed on time as promised). (Continued)

In essence, the action plans become the project charter for SSM. They are not part of a separate document but are actually incorporated into the strategic plans of the organization. They identify the problem and the steps to solve it, set responsibilities, provide a timetable, and estimate associated costs, all of which are directed toward achieving the predefined objectives.

One additional benefit of SSM is that it ensures that all Six Sigma deployments are strategically consistent with the organization's direction. These deployments are made under the disciplined direction of the organization's strategic plan and in response to the VOM. There is an unbroken line of communication from the market to specific areas of the organization. The VOM directs value enhancement and revenue growth. There is no helter-skelter use of Six Sigma and its resources in areas where there is no strategic interest or benefit to the organization.

Budget and Forecasts

Each action will have direct costs associated with its completion. These should be detailed and added to determine the actual cost of the plan. Based on market share objectives or unit sales objectives, forecasts can be made of revenue flows. The difference between these revenue flows and the costs of the plan represents a basis for determining the return on investment of the plan. If done properly, the plan should provide a positive return.

The competitive planning process, integrated with the DMAIC process, is an important tool for SSM. In essence, it becomes a detailed project charter for SSM. It provides a structured approach for accomplishing market share and revenue goals while at the same time providing financial accountability for SSM. This accountability enhances the credibility of the role of marketing within the organization. Too often marketing critics claim that marketing is a cost center and not a revenue generator. SSM refutes these claims by providing a fact-based approach for achieving revenue and performance goals in an accountable manner.

Chapter 4 begins the discussion of the modified DMAIC approach that provides the analytical structure for SSM.

4

Define: Identifying Marketing Opportunities for Business Growth

The structural problem-solving architecture of SSM is a modified DMAIC process. It is modified to accommodate three major elements: a market focus, SSM's reliance on customer value and the requisite value tools, and a concentration on market share growth.

The define stage of SSM (see Figure 4.1) represents a departure from both the orthodoxy of traditional marketing and the DMAIC approach of conventional Six Sigma. Conventional marketing strategy typically relies on market segmentation, a unidimensional approach, as the initial step in strategy development. The premise is that market segments, if properly defined, evince a more homogeneous buying behavior. This is correct as far as it goes. However, it can be refined by adding another dimension—one focusing not only on similar types of buyers but also on specific product lines that these market segments buy. This sharpens the focus significantly, reducing the variability of behavior even more, and ultimately producing a VOM that is significantly more accurate. Moreover, taken together, the two elements of markets and products represent the very factors that produce revenues and market share—a principal performance goal of SSM. This linkage to revenues is not present in typical marketing segmentation.

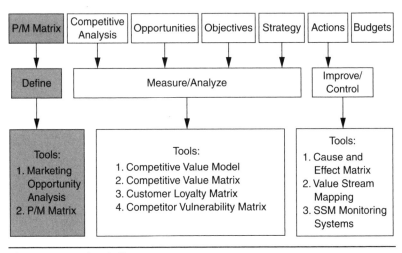

SSM: An integrative process

| P/M Matrix | Competitive Analysis | Opportunities | Objectives | Strategy | Actions | Budgets |

| Define | Measure/Analyze | Improve/Control |

Tools:
1. Marketing Opportunity Analysis
2. P/M Matrix

Tools:
1. Competitive Value Model
2. Competitive Value Matrix
3. Customer Loyalty Matrix
4. Competitor Vulnerability Matrix

Tools:
1. Cause and Effect Matrix
2. Value Stream Mapping
3. SSM Monitoring Systems

Figure 4.1 The define stage.

Regarding the other point of departure, Six Sigma typically uses the define stage to identify and clarify the objectives and value of a project. However, at this point in the execution of the SSM methodology, there is no project since the analysis stage has not identified a value performance issue within a specific product/market. SSM is market focused and value driven. Accordingly, the define stage is used to focus on one or more specific product/markets to assess their importance from a growth standpoint for the organization and set the stage for identifying value-based opportunities. The assessment of P/M importance ensures that the organization is not investing resources in areas that have little, if any, economic importance to the organization. This single step greatly enhances the return on investment produced by SSM. Subsequent stages in the SSM model analyze these opportunities for enhancing revenues and market share, including Six Sigma projects to sharpen value delivery processes.

The product/market approach forms the basis of the organization's competitive strategy, ensuring that all SSM deployments are consistent with the organization's competitive strategy.

PRODUCT/MARKETS (P/Ms)

Six Sigma marketers look at the idea of market segmentation somewhat differently than their more traditional marketing counterparts. As indicated earlier, in addition to market segments they add in another dimension, product lines, to produce a P/M Matrix. The P/M Matrix is the principal tool used in the define stage of SSM. The goal of SSM is to increase top-line revenues and market share. It uses customer value as its strategic metric because of its strong linkage to revenues and market share (see Chapter 2). The P/M Matrix aligns the two factors that create revenues for the enterprise: the products or services that the organization sells and the markets that buy them. This provides a laserlike focus not only on the buyers but on the products they buy, identifying the two components that define the competitive arenas in which the organization chooses to compete.

PRODUCT LINES

Product lines are groups of similar and interchangeable products as defined by the market. Products are not interchangeable between product lines. For example, home mortgages are not substitutes for checking accounts. Similarly, for farmers, tractors are not substitutes for balers. For consumers, cookies are not substitutes for vegetables. On the other hand, within the mortgage product line, consumers can choose 10-year, 15-year, 40-year, or even adjustable mortgages. For the farmer, there are different horsepower tractors within the tractor product line. For the shopper, there are a number of different types of cookies within the cookie product line. Products within the same product line may come in different sizes, colors, and weights, even though some sizes, colors, or weights may be more preferable to some buyers than others. Without clearly defined product lines, analysis and subsequent action become hazy and less focused—resulting in less effectiveness and lower efficiency. Increased effectiveness and increased efficiency are two key goals of SSM.

A key element of the product line definition has to do with how customers or buyers of the line see the product line. Product lines should be defined from the market standpoint and not based on engineering similarities or cost reporting. A cohort of mine recounted a situation where a major manufacturer of heavy equipment came up with the idea of a Century Line comprising smaller types of equipment of less than 100 horsepower. Unfortunately, the Century Line idea appeared to be lost on the buyer. No one came in to see or asked about Century Line products; they came in to see small wheel loaders and other small horsepower gear. Defining product lines internally can lead to unnecessary and debilitating confusion in the marketplace.

How the market defines value will change from product line to product line. For example, farmers will have a different value definition for tractors than they will for balers. Similarly, the definition of value for a mortgage product is completely different from that of a checking account. Focusing on a properly defined product line reduces the variance of evaluations (a notion most Six Sigma practitioners are familiar with), leading to a better and clearer understanding of how they define value. CTQs are more clearly defined. Less variance produces more highly actionable information, making actions more effective and more efficient by providing more exacting metrics.

MARKET SEGMENTS

The second element of a P/M Matrix is market segments, or groups of buyers with similar buying needs. Segments offer the same benefit of focus as product lines in that they reduce the variance that exists across the entire market, providing an added clarity to understanding buying motives and CTQs. There are essentially two questions to be answered regarding market segments: (1) how to segment, and (2) which segments to target.

How to Segment

There are a number of ways in which markets can be segmented: demographics, psychographics, heavy versus light usage, geography, attitude, and size of customer, to name a few. A key rule regarding market segments is that they must be "findable." Findable refers to the ease of actually identifying customers and being able to correctly sort them into groups or segments. Here's an example. Demographics are a common segmentation basis simply because it is easy to sort customers according to gender or age or region of a country. Some segmentation schemes are based on elaborate techniques that can sort customers according to abstract factors such as attitude. This is fine if, and only if, customers with one attitude can be readily identified and separated from those with different attitudes. The best test of a good segmentation approach is to put yourself in the following situation: A customer walks into your place of business and you ask that customer a couple of questions. On the basis of the customer's answers, can you put the customer into the proper segment? If not, your segmentation scheme is not "findable." Segments should also be substantial (large enough to have economic potential; after all, the basic segment is a single customer), quantifiable (countable), and easy to access (communicate with).

Many organizations confuse product lines with market segments. At one workshop for a group of manufacturers, I asked how many companies relied on segmentation. A couple of hands went up. I asked one participant who had raised his hand how his company segments. He responded that his company has a locomotive segment, a bus segment, and a truck segment and followed up with the comment that segmentation does not work. Small wonder—his segments were product lines, not people with similar needs who buy products. Customers buy locomotives, buses, and trucks. To my knowledge, locomotives don't buy anything.

Which Segments to Target

The answer to the second question—which segments to target—is equally important. Choosing the wrong segments increases the risk of an ineffective and inefficient execution of strategy, resulting in lower probabilities of reaching targeted share and revenue objectives. Some segments that have been identified will not be worth investing in. There is little likelihood of achieving desired revenue and share objectives, and it will not be worth the investment. These segments might be too small, have low growth, be competitively intense, and so forth, or the organization may not be capable of competing effectively within the segment. This requires the organization to assess the opportunity that each segment offers. SSM uses two factors to determine the opportunity that a segment offers: (1) the attractiveness of the segment, and (2) the organization's ability to compete within that segment.

Segment Attractiveness

Segment attractiveness can be measured using a number of metrics:

- Segment size (units/dollars)
- Segment growth rate (units/dollars)
- Post-sales revenues (parts and service)
- Competitive intensity
- Other metrics specific to individual industries

There are undoubtedly a number of factors that when weighted in terms of their importance to the organization will have an overall attractiveness score. The weighting will put these combined factors on a scale of 1 to 10, with 10 being highly attractive.

Ability to Compete

The ability to compete is likewise a multidimensional factor that may comprise the following:

- Financial resources necessary to compete
- Distribution capabilities
- Product breadth and width
- Capability of personnel
- Other metrics specific to individual industries

Like attractiveness, these can be compiled into a weighted dimension ranging from 1 to 10, with 10 being a strong ability to compete.

Putting these two dimensions together produces the Market Opportunity Matrix shown in Figure 4.2. This matrix was

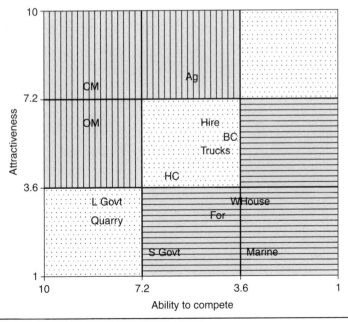

Figure 4.2 The Market Opportunity Matrix.

generated for a large heavy-equipment dealer and shows the evaluation of the different segments it serves.

The matrix aligns the ability to compete dimension on the horizontal axis and the attractiveness dimension on the vertical axis. There are three areas of the matrix:

- Those segments falling into the high attractiveness/strong ability to compete area (vertical shading)

- Those segments falling into the moderate attractiveness/ moderate ability to compete area (dotted shading)

- Those segments falling into the low attractiveness/weak ability to compete area (horizontal shading)

Clearly, those segments falling into the high attractiveness/strong ability to compete area are the most desirable from a targeting perspective. In the example shown in Figure 4.2, these are contract miners (CM), owner miners (OM), and agriculture (Ag). By definition, the segments within this area of the matrix are those with high economic or strategic value and those the organization has a strong ability to compete in. Those falling into the moderate attractiveness/moderate ability to compete area (hire [rental], building construction [BC], trucks, heavy construction [HC], local government [L Govt], and quarry) are the next most desirable, while those falling into the low attractiveness/weak ability to compete area (warehouse [WHouse], forestry [For], state government [S Govt], and marine) are the least desirable.

This type of analysis is important for a couple of reasons. Again, it requires bringing together personnel who are familiar with the different markets and their value to the organization. It requires team members to *prove* the attractiveness of the segment and *prove* that the organization has what it takes to compete effectively within each segment. Simply declaring a segment or market to be attractive is insufficient. Similarly, saying the organization has a strong ability to compete should not be accepted outright. The Market Opportunity Analysis requires facts—the scores on the two criteria. These can and should be challenged and proof offered. This is designed to eliminate agendas and lore as the principal means of targeting. It introduces a level of accountability to the targeting process that, in many organizations, did not exist. Finally, it provides a means for monitoring changes in the potential attractiveness of the segments and the organization's ability to compete that will change over time.

PRIORITIZING MARKET OPPORTUNITIES

The define stage in SSM has the objective of defining/identifying and prioritizing market opportunities that represent solid growth options for the organization. The principal tool in the define stage is the P/M Matrix. As indicated earlier, the P/M Matrix aligns the two factors that are involved in generating revenue and market share for the organization—the organization's product and services and the people who buy them. Revenue growth and market share growth are the twin objectives of SSM. The P/M Matrix has a huge advantage over simple segmentation since it not only focuses on the people who have similar buying needs (segments) but also identifies the products or services they use. This decreases the variance even more so. Buyers' needs are more closely clustered about the mean, resulting in less deviation from the mean and clearer and more accurate metrics. Consider the added power of measures that focus not only on a segment of buyers but also on the specific products and services they buy. The effectiveness and efficiency of SSM programs is enhanced by understanding how this segment buying a specific product defines value. If we are focusing on farmers, what equipment are they evaluating—tractors, balers, manure spreaders? Failure to include this product-line level of focus adds a distortion to the evaluation process and degree of variance that makes reliance of statistical methodology less effective. We will obtain much better information if we ask farmers to evaluate specific product lines as opposed to "ag equipment."

Figure 4.3 depicts a generalized P/M Matrix. Across the top of the matrix are the different market segments that the organization *can* serve. It may not serve all these segments, but they exist and represent a certain degree of potential opportunity, some greater than others. Down the vertical axis of the matrix are the organization's product lines. Included in this list are product lines that the organization may not offer but may be offered by competitors. The intersection of the segments with the product lines enumerates the different marketing opportunities presented to the organization. These opportunities take the form of providing product A to market A or product B to market D.

The question facing the Six Sigma marketer is, "Which of these opportunities represents the best option for growth of the enterprise?" This involves an evaluation of each cell or product/market using specific evaluation criteria. These criteria might include size of the product/market, growth of the product/market, competitive intensity of the product/market, the organization's current market share of the product/market, and lost sales within the product/market. There are others, of course, and it is

Market / Product	Market A	Market B	Market C	Market D			Total
Product A							
Product B							
Product C							
Total							

Figure 4.3 A generalized P/M Matrix.

up to the Six Sigma marketer to identify those criteria that do the best job in terms of evaluating the market opportunity for the organization.

Each product/market is evaluated using the same set of criteria, producing a basis on which the different opportunities can be prioritized. This evaluation process is made simpler by the marketing opportunity assessment made earlier. The organization, using the Marketing Opportunity Matrix, will have already identified the most desirable segments or markets. All that remains is to identify the specific product lines that the organization will use to compete within these markets.

Not all product/market opportunities facing the organization will be worth investing in. Some will be better growth opportunities than others, and it is up to the Six Sigma marketer to identify which are the best. The organization may choose to invest in all the "good" opportunities or just a few. This judgment is constrained by resources such as economic and human capital, distribution capabilities, and so forth. The organization is free to choose where it will compete, and it will use an informed data-driven, fact-based approach to make this choice. This eliminates agendas and corporate lore as a basis for targeting specific market opportunities. From a managerial perspective, the issue is, "How do we increase revenues from segment A that is buying product A?" This is quite different from the question, "How do we increase revenues from segment A?"

Each product/market that is targeted will have its own set of competitors that may differ from other product/markets. Each product/market will have a different definition of value than other product/markets. Here's an example from the financial services industry. A commercial bank generated the abbreviated P/M Matrix shown in Figure 4.4.

The bank targeted the credit cards/singles product/market and the loans (mortgage)/full nest 1 (households with young

Product \ Market	Singles	Single parents	Full nest 1	Full nest 2	Empty nest	Sole survivor
Savings						
Transaction						
Investment				Competitive value proposition?		
Loans						
Credit cards						

Figure 4.4   P/M Matrix for a commercial bank.

children) product/market. The basis of its segmentation was lifestyle, noting that customers' financial needs varied depending on the current stage of their life cycle. The competitors within the product/market of credit cards/singles include other commercial banks, car companies, mortgage brokers, and other non-banking entities. Within the mortgage/full nest 1 product/market, competitors include other commercial banks, automobile companies, credit unions, investment banks, and other non-banking entities. In other words, the bank's assuming that it was simply competing against other commercial banks would be a big mistake. Moreover, customers choosing a credit card would define credit card value differently than those who are evaluating mortgage options. Assuming a single definition of value would produce highly ineffective and inefficient actions.

Here's another example of how an enterprise looked at its market opportunities. Figure 4.5 shows the P/M Matrix for a large heavy-equipment dealer.

This organization used the Market Opportunity Analysis shown in Figure 4.2 and an applications-based segmentation approach. The vertically striped cells are those markets in which the dealer has a strong ability to compete and are highly attractive. The cells with dots are the average—average attractiveness and average ability to compete. Finally, the horizontally

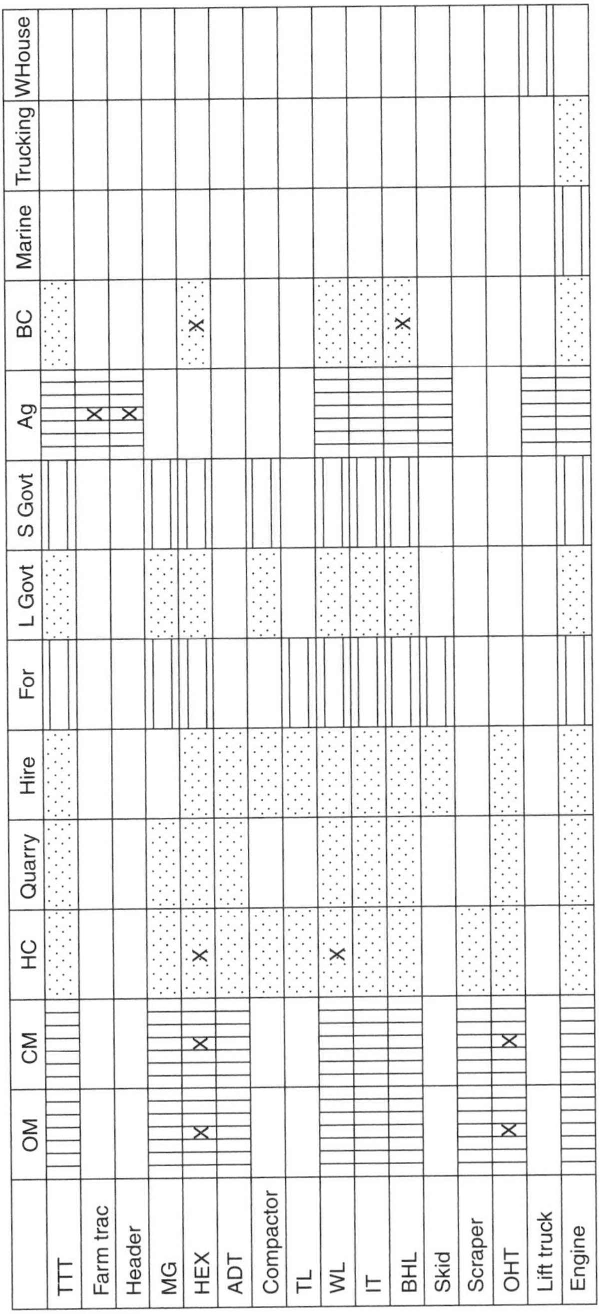

	OM	CM	HC	Quarry	Hire	For	L Govt	S Govt	Ag	BC	Marine	Trucking	WHouse
TTT													
Farm trac									X				
Header									X				
MG													
HEX	X	X	X							X			
ADT													
Compactor													
TL													
WL			X							X			
IT													
BHL													
Skid													
Scraper													
OHT	X	X											
Lift truck													
Engine													

Figure 4.5   P/M Matrix for a heavy-equipment dealer.

striped cells are markets in which the dealer has a weaker ability to compete and are unattractive. These different segments or applications are shown across the top, for example, mining (OM—owner miners, and CM—contract miners), heavy construction, quarry, hire (rental), and so forth. Listed on the side of the matrix are the different product lines offered by the dealer. These include farm tractors, headers (combines), motor graders, hydraulic excavators, and so forth. The intersection of the product lines with the segments identifies the potential opportunities the dealer can target as part of its strategy. This matrix identified 208 opportunities for the dealer, each providing different levels of economic benefits to the dealer. Of course, the dealer could not take advantage of all the opportunities even if it wanted to. Some cells are not viable. For example, there is little opportunity selling articulated dump trucks to marine customers, or hydraulic excavators to foresters. After eliminating the nonviable opportunities, the dealer used its strategic criteria to identify the 10 best opportunities for growth. In fact, these 10 opportunities (indicated with an X) generate 80 percent of its total revenues. Does this mean that it will not do business with those customers in product/markets not selected? No. The dealer will sell them any piece of equipment they want. But it will not *invest* in these product/markets, because they offer little opportunity for growth. They are the options that are low growth, small in size, competitively intense, and so forth.

The P/M Matrix allows the enterprise to focus on specific market opportunities for maximal effectiveness and efficiency, an important goal of SSM. Underlying the use of the P/M Matrix is the idea that the organization cannot be everything to everyone. It is a market-focused approach that is not driven or contaminated by internal guesses and agendas.

In the *iSixSigma* study (Goeke, Marx, and Reidenbach 2008) cited earlier, of the 951 Six Sigma professionals interviewed, 55 percent noted challenges regarding getting appropriate customer information. Underlying this challenge was the concern about identifying the right customer. Equipping Six Sigma marketers with the P/M Matrix eliminates this problem.

SSM begins the DMAIC process with a modified define stage—one that defines the specific product/market opportunities in which the organization chooses to compete. This automatically aligns Six Sigma with the marketing strategy, ensuring that Six Sigma deployments and resources are invested in a way that is consistent with overall strategies.

REFERENCE

Goeke, Reginald, Michael Marx, and Eric Reidenbach. 2008. "Hearing Voices: How Businesses Listen to the Customer." *iSixSigma Magazine*, July/August, 31–38.

5

Measure: Defining Value for Targeted Product/Markets

A basic premise of SSM is that for every product/market targeted, based on the opportunity it provides the organization, there will be a unique definition of value. This value definition is represented in the Competitive Value Model—the principal tool for the measure stage of SSM (see Figure 5.1).

The value model captures the VOM and becomes the information platform that drives the subsequent stages of SSM. Accordingly, it provides yet another point of departure from conventional Six Sigma methodology, which relies on the VOC. That the VOM is a relatively new concept is reflected in the *iSixSigma* survey (Goeke, Marx, and Reidenbach 2008) of Six Sigma practitioners, where only 16 percent indicated that their company's process improvement projects were driven by the VOM. Of the remaining respondents, 37 percent indicated that they relied on the VOC, while 58 percent relied on the voice of the business (defined in the study as so-called internal customers).

The VOM is a significantly more powerful concept than the traditional VOC. The VOC captures information from the

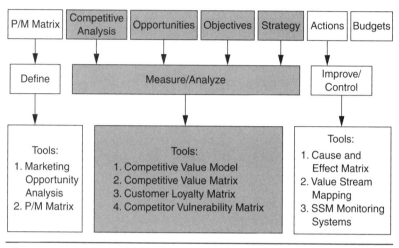

Figure 5.1   The measure/analyze stages.

organization's own customer base but does not include information from competitors' customers. Because the goal of SSM is increased market share through value enhancement, the traditional reliance on VOC is inadequate. The VOC cannot account for the dynamism of competition that drives changes in market share. Moreover, lacking a comparative capacity, the VOC can be misleading. Here's an example. Suppose you find out that your customers give you a value rating of 8.2 on a 10-point scale. Is this good? Is it sufficient to attract new customers? Now what if you find out that your two key competitors received an 8.7 and a 9.2 on this same value dimension? How does that change your answers to the questions of whether this is good and whether this is sufficient to attract new customers?

There are two components to the measure stage of SSM. The first is the actual measurement component—how do you obtain the information? This was cited by Six Sigma practitioners in the *iSixSigma* survey as one of the most crucial challenges facing the community. Comments such as the following characterized the nature of this challenge (36):

- Getting useable information from the people who count

- Getting a representative sample from the most appropriate customer segment

- How to accurately define and choose the "right" measurements

The second component is how to interpret the data to provide a meaningful and relevant basis for action. First, how do you obtain the value information?

CAPTURING THE VOM

There is a standard process for capturing the VOM. Some organizations will be able to do this internally, while others will have to outsource this activity. It is not the intention of this chapter to provide a thorough discussion of the research process. This is explained elsewhere in great detail (see Reidenbach 2009). The current intention is to provide an overview that touches on the high points of the process. The VOM process is outlined as follows:

- Identify critical product/markets

- Conduct focus groups

- Develop the questionnaire

- Create the sample

- Field the questionnaire

- Create model

Identify Critical Product/Markets

The process begins with identifying the critical product/markets, which was the subject of Chapter 4. This occurs in the define stage of SSM. The P/M Matrix simplifies this task and uses a fact-based approach rather than one driven by agendas. Product/markets cannot be selected without referral to the specific criteria used to evaluate them.

Conduct Focus Groups

Focus groups are classified as an exploratory data collection methodology. They are made up of a small group of targeted buyers, both your customers and those of your competitors. The purpose of the focus group is to find out what questions need to be included in the questionnaire that will be developed from the group sessions. The group usually numbers between 8 and 12, but there is no hard and fast rule as to the number. In some markets, 8–12 customers may actually make up the entire market, so the focus group represents a census. These groups are used to understand, on a qualitative basis, how customers (yours and your competitors') define value within this product/market. These are open and free-ranging discussions of experiences, wish lists, practices (both best and worst), and other relevant experiential bases of eliciting how these customers define value. Much of the discussion focuses on the quality component of value—what constitutes quality. The moderator will record these sessions so that they can be reviewed in depth at a later time. It is critical that the moderator keep the group on track and relevant. A sample focus group outline is appended to this chapter as a reference.

There are a couple of key factors that will determine the success of the groups. First is the screening process. Make sure that the participants have experience with the product/service and are part of the market segment that is targeted. There is nothing worse than trying to discuss a concept such as value with people who have no experience with the product or service.

Second, since the focus group is used to understand what questions need to be asked in the questionnaire, make sure that the attributes and potential questions that come out of the focus group are actionable and germane to the issue at hand. Again, populating a questionnaire with a number of questions that have little actionability is a real waste of time and dollars.

Third, conduct as many focus groups as necessary. When you start to hear the same things over again, this usually means you've done enough groups. Redundancy is a sign that you've gotten as much as you can from the groups. At a minimum, conduct at least two groups.

Fourth, do not fall into the trap of believing that the groups are providing definitive information. Again, your goal is to identify the questions you need to ask during the survey phase. It is tempting to think that the focus groups are providing definitive information when usually they are not. Many Six Sigma practitioners recommend focus groups as the sole information source for project identification and execution. This means you might be basing your Six Sigma deployment on what 16 or so people are saying. If the Six Sigma project is an internal one, this may be adequate. However, for the purpose of SSM and its market focus, this is too small a sample to extrapolate from and can result in misleading conclusions that will impede any further efforts to fix problems or leverage strengths. It is extremely difficult to identify CTQs from these groups. That will come later.

Fifth, be sure to capture in the buyers' language what they mean by a particular evaluative attribute. You may be surprised that they speak a different language than your engineers, quality people, or technicians. I recall a situation where a marketing group was talking about "machine reliability." I had reported that the buyers used machine reliability in a way that was different from the way the company did. The marketing manager replied, "This is crap. They don't know what they are talking about!" Believe me, they do.

One final word of caution: Because of the relatively low cost of focus groups and the speed with which information can be collected, too many organizations rely on them as their principal source of information. This is dangerous and akin to arguing from an *n* of 1. There is seldom a sufficient sample size to extrapolate to the larger P/M universe with any reliability. Bad information leads to bad decisions. This is one place where some information is not necessarily better than none. For every targeted product/market, you will need to conduct focus groups.

Develop the Questionnaire

The output from the focus groups becomes the input for the questionnaire. Again, the purpose is not to equip the reader with a comprehensive set of skills to become a market researcher— just a better judge and a more informed potential buyer of research.

While there are a number of questionnaire vehicles (for example, telephone, mail, face-to-face, Internet), it is important that the questionnaire get to the proper person. Mail questionnaires do not provide this capability and can be filled out by anyone (secretaries, the new guy, and so forth). This can clearly impact the quality of the information.

Telephone surveys, face-to-face surveys, and Internet surveys provide a basis for screening the potential respondent to ensure that you are speaking with the correct individual. Accordingly, they are recommended over mail questionnaires, even though they may cost more. Figure 5.2 provides a summary of the strengths and weaknesses of the different types of survey techniques.

You will want to take into account the different survey types—their strengths and weaknesses—when considering which vehicle to use. Again, the reader is referred to Reidenbach (2009) for a more thorough discussion of these factors. Of course, such issues as the availability of telephone numbers, Internet addresses, costs, and the amount of information

Method Factor	Face-to-face	Phone	Mail	Internet
Cost/completed interview	High	Moderate	Low	Low
Content flexibility	Yes	No	Yes	Yes
Speed	Slow	Fast	Slow	Fast
Potential bias	Higher	Higher	Lower	Lower
Representativeness	Low	Moderate	Moderate	Moderate
Flexibility of programming	High	High	Low	High
Amount of information/ interviewing time	Low	Low	Moderate	High
Accuracy	Moderate	Moderate	High	High

Figure 5.2 A comparison of four survey techniques.

to be collected will help determine the best and most cost-effective approach.

Here are several considerations when developing a questionnaire or working with a market research firm. First, make sure that there is a provision for randomizing the questions. This is easily done using either telephone or Internet surveys. Randomization of questions takes out any order effects that might be accidentally built into the questionnaire. As an example of order effects, some questionnaires will group the questions into distribution questions, product questions, pricing questions, and so forth. This organization may unintentionally "format the respondent's mental disk" in such a way as to generate responses that are correlated. By randomizing the questions, this likelihood is reduced.

Second, don't be afraid to ask the same question in different ways. This ensures the reliability of the information. Multiple measures are more statistically reliable than single-item questions. Often brevity is the guiding principle in questionnaire development and not information integrity.

Third, how many scale points should you use? Should the questionnaire use a 5-, 7-, or 10-point scale? A number of studies have been conducted that have revealed that there is little difference in results when using different scales. What is important is to get away from the overly simplistic yes/no nominal level measurement. There is very little that can be done with this simplistic measurement other than to categorize or count responses. Instead, try to operate at the interval or ordered metric level of measurement. These are the scales that employ the 7- or 10-point scales. These are premised on the idea that the intervals are equal, thus allowing more sophisticated statistical manipulations of the data. These scales can be input into factor analytic programs, regression analysis, and discriminant analysis—all of the more sophisticated multivariate techniques—and can yield significantly more and powerful information. Figure 5.3 illustrates the different levels of measurement and what can be done with them.

How do you anchor the scales? *Anchors* are the words attached to the end points of the scales. Common anchors include

Level of measurement	Example	Mathematical operation
Nominal	Yes/no questions	Categorize, count
Ordinal	Ranking questions—Which is your favorite, next favorite, etc.	List in order of magnitude of property—1st, 2nd, 3rd, etc.
Interval	Scaled questions—3-, 5-, 7-, 10-point scales anchored with performance, satisfaction, etc.	Most statistical operations—adding, subtracting, averaging, etc.
Ratio	Actual zero point—dollars, temperature (Kelvin)	All

Figure 5.3 Levels of measurement.

"strongly agree/strongly disagree," "very satisfied/very dissatisfied," "like very much/dislike very much," and so on. They are supposed to be polar opposites at each end of the scale.

Because SSM seeks to improve performance, scales anchored with "excellent performance/poor performance" provide powerful insight into value advantages and disadvantages. They direct attention to those areas where the market says performance improvement is necessary. There is little interpretive confusion in their results. Moreover, how well your organization *performs* on specific attributes can be directly compared with the performance of your competitors, along with advantages targeted for leveraging and disadvantages focused on for improving performance. Performance, after all, is the competitive coin of the realm.

Some questionnaires include not only performance measures but also corresponding importance questions. Respondents are asked to evaluate the importance of each attribute and their company's performance on that attribute. This approach is called *stated importance*. The downside of this approach is the potential correlated effects of the two responses and the increased size of the questionnaire and the time it takes to administer it. Response fatigue can set in, resulting in incomplete responses.

There is another approach for determining importance—*derived importance*. This is generated through multiple regression types of techniques where the regression model creates b weights (b), or beta weights (β), that indicate the relative importance of each independent variable. Derived importance addresses the two major weaknesses associated with the stated importance approach.

Questionnaires can be administered as either blind or identified. Blind questionnaires increase the likelihood of reducing any halo effects that might be associated with a particular brand or company. On the other hand, identifying the source of the survey may increase the willingness of people to respond to it. This may be particularly helpful in transactional measurements where you are trying to assess how *your* customers evaluated *your* performance (see Chapter 8).

Create the Sample

Creating the sample is a particularly complex issue that is addressed in significantly greater detail by Reidenbach (2009). There are two issues: how many people to sample and what kind of sampling approach to use.

Figure 5.4 shows the different options relative to the error rate and the level of confidence selected.

Most surveys are conducted with a confidence level of 95 percent and an error rate of ±5 percent. This means that if you were to conduct the survey an infinite number of times, 95 times out of 100 (confidence level) your estimates would be within + or − 5 percent (error rate) of the true parameter. Changing these options, higher level of confidence or lower error rate, increases the size of the sample and, of course, the cost.

The type of sample, random or nonrandom, is somewhat more problematic. In surveying markets, you will need a dependable list of consumers or buyers with corresponding telephone numbers, addresses, or Internet addresses. The sample that you draw is random to the list but not necessarily to the market. Most survey work proceeds on the premise that the list is also representative of the market. Obviously, the better the lists (the more representative of the population), the greater the randomness of the results. Accordingly, most sampling processes approach randomness instead of guaranteeing it. This is different from the typical sampling done with Six Sigma projects that focuses on a production run. Greater control means greater randomness.

Quota sampling is an often used technique. For example, if market share estimates are known, you might want to break

Population size	Error—95% confidence				Error—99% confidence			
	5.00%	3.50%	2.50%	1.00%	5.00%	3.50%	2.50%	1.00%
10	10	10	10	10	10	10	10	10
20	19	20	20	20	20	19	20	20
30	28	29	29	30	29	29	30	30
50	44	47	48	50	47	48	49	50
75	63	69	72	74	67	71	73	75
100	80	89	94	99	87	93	96	99
150	108	126	137	148	122	135	142	149
200	132	160	177	196	154	174	186	198
250	152	190	215	244	182	211	229	246
300	169	217	251	291	207	246	270	295
400	196	265	318	384	250	309	348	391
500	217	306	377	475	285	365	421	485
600	234	340	432	565	315	416	490	579
700	248	370	481	653	341	462	554	672
800	260	396	526	739	363	503	615	763
1,000	278	440	606	906	399	575	727	943
1,200	291	474	674	1067	427	636	827	1119
1,500	306	515	759	1297	460	712	959	1376
2,000	322	563	869	1655	498	808	1141	1785
2,500	333	597	952	1984	524	879	1288	2173
3,500	346	641	1068	2565	558	977	1510	2890
5,000	357	678	1176	3288	586	1066	1734	3842
7,500	365	710	1275	4211	610	1147	1960	5165
10,000	370	727	1332	4899	622	1193	2098	6239
25,000	378	760	1448	6939	646	1285	2399	9972
50,000	381	772	1491	8056	655	1318	2520	12455
75,000	382	776	1506	8514	658	1330	2563	13583
100,000	383	778	1513	8762	659	1336	2585	14227
250,000	384	782	1527	9248	662	1347	2626	15555
500,000	384	783	1532	9423	663	1350	2640	16055
1,000,000	384	783	1534	9512	663	1352	2647	16317
2,500,000	384	784	1536	9567	663	1353	2651	16478
10,000,000	384	784	1536	9594	663	1354	2653	16560
100,000,000	384	784	1537	9603	663	1354	2654	16584
300,000,000	384	784	1537	9603	663	1354	2654	16586

Figure 5.4 Sample size calculator.

Source: The Research Advisors (2006).

your overall sample down into the market share proportions. Surveyors are instructed to fill the quotas. Quota sampling assumes that the quotas will be large enough for the central limit theorem to kick in where n (the sample size) is large enough to allow the sample mean to approximate the universe mean and the sample standard deviation to approach the universe standard deviation.

Field the Questionnaire

Once the questionnaire is developed and the sampling plan created, the survey is fielded. It's prudent to test the survey prior to full fielding to make sure that the questions are understood and that the questionnaire has no problems. Fielding can be by telephone, mail, personal interview, or the Internet. Once the data have been collected, the Competitive Value Model can be constructed.

CREATE THE COMPETITIVE VALUE MODEL

The second aspect of the measurement component of SSM involves interpreting the data. This means understanding how the product/market defines value.

Creating the Competitive Value Model involves using several multivariate techniques, most notably factor analysis and multiple regression analysis. Once the data are collected, they are input into a factor analytic procedure that sorts the responses on the basis of response similarity. This creates buckets of attributes that have a commonality and a latency. Each bucket is then analyzed as to what this commonality is and then named on the basis of its commonality. Factor analysis is often referred to as latent dimension analysis since it produces groups of attributes that form a dimension revealing a meaning that is greater and more important than any single attribute. An example will help illustrate this property. Consider the attributes shown in

Figure 5.5, which were used in a value analysis of the wireless telecom industry. These attributes were extracted during several focus groups of buyers within the targeted product/market and randomized during the telephone survey process.

Seven buckets of attributes were identified by the factor analysis:

- Product features
- Technical competence
- Customer focus
- Billing
- Image
- Price
- Value

Figure 5.5 shows the structure of the different buckets.

Under each factor name are the attributes that compose that factor and give name to it. These factors are the latent dimensions that reveal something larger than the individual attributes. Some factors are readily self-explanatory, such as billing or price. Others have to be examined to understand the nature of the commonality that underlies them; for example, customer focus. These attributes appeared to speak to understanding the customer's business, treating the customer like a valued business partner, responsiveness to needs, and so forth. Collectively, the attributes appeared to describe what the organization chose to call "customer focus." These labels are subjective—open to the interpretation of the analyst—but their importance is paramount. These factors become candidate value drivers (quality, price, and image) and potential CTQs (product features, technical competence, customer focus, and billing). They are referred to as "potential" since the next step in creating the value model determines their actuality.

Product features
Offering features that meet your organization's needs
Offering features that are simple to use
Offering consistently reliable products and services
Providing a variety of accessories for their products

Technical competence
Call clarity
Providing service without dropped or disconnected calls
Getting calls through on the first try, for example, no system-busy or fast busy signals
The quality of calls made while outside your organization's home service area
Being a company that provides service coverage that meets your organization's needs

Customer focus
Treating your organization like a valued business partner
Being responsive to your organization's questions and service needs
Being a company that consistently delivers above and beyond expectations
Company reps having a positive attitude
Company reps promptly making changes to your organization's service when you request them
Company reps resolving problems to your satisfaction
After the sale, company reps resolving problems the first time you call
Company reps accurately representing products and services.
Company reps providing clear and concise explanations about the bill
Company reps providing timely training on how to use the products and services
After the sale, the ease with which you can reach the right person to solve your organization's problem
After the sale, Customer Service that is easy to do business with
Being a company that provides business solutions to satisfy all your organization's communications needs
Being a company that understands the needs of your business
Proactive communication on promotions or new product and service offerings
Providing easy access to products, service, and/or accessories at a convenient retail location

Figure 5.5   Attribute components.

Billing
Bills being easy to understand
Bills being accurate
No hidden/unexpected charges on bill

Reputation
Being a company that is easy to do business with
Being a company you can trust
Being technologically innovative
Being a company that stands behind the service it sells
Being customer-focused
Being a company that keeps its commitments
Being a company whose logo you would be proud to wear or display
Being a company that does what it says it's going to do

PRICE
Monthly price charged for service
Charges for calls made <u>outside</u> your local service area
Offering a variety of bundled services to meet your organization's needs
Prices charged for optional features, such as voice mail or text messaging
Offering service pricing plans that meet your organization's needs
Flexibility to change price plans
Renewing contract is a fair and simple process

VALUE
The value your organization receives, considering the <u>quality of service</u> that _____ provides your organization and the <u>price your organization pays for that service</u>
The value your organization receives, considering all of the <u>benefits</u> that _____ provides your organization and the <u>price your organization pays for those benefits</u>

Figure 5.5 Attribute components. (Continued)

Another important aspect of the factors has to do with a statistical issue called *multicollinearity*. In multiple regression, this condition occurs when the independent variables are more highly correlated with each other than they are with the dependent variable. Multicollinearity can confound the outcome of the regression model, since it can over- or understate the importance of the beta weights, producing misleading and erroneous results.

A two-stage regression analysis produced the market-based value model shown in Figure 5.6.

THE COMPETITIVE VALUE MODEL

Figure 5.6 illustrates the Competitive Value Model. There are two components to the model: the explanatory component and the managerial component.

The Explanatory Component

Value is the dependent dimension (a linear combination of the value attributes shown in Figure 5.5). The task of the model is to capture the degree to which value is explained using the three value drivers (Customer Quality Index [CQI] or quality,

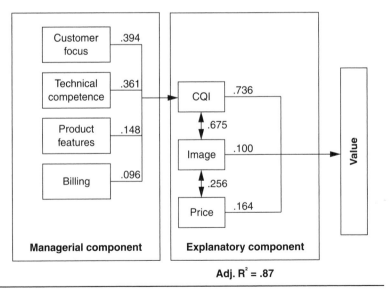

Figure 5.6 Competitive Value Model: Wireless telecom.

image, and price). CQI comprises the potential CTQs (product features, technical competence, customer focus, and billing), weighted in terms of their relative importance to value. The degree of explanatory power is revealed in the R^2 statistic (coefficient of determination interpreted as a correlation). R^2 is a measure of association and can vary between 0 and 1.0. The larger the R^2, the greater the explanatory power of the model. In this case, the R^2 is .87, a relatively high value indicating a high degree of explanatory power. In other words, the model does a good job of explaining how the market defines value.

The values adjacent to each value driver indicate the relative importance of each driver in explaining value. In this case, quality has the biggest impact (.736), followed by price (.164) and then image (.100). This is important to know because a positive change in quality will have a significantly bigger impact on a change in value than a change in price or image. This component of the model provides the first level of focus for subsequent action—a focus on quality as opposed to price. This will eliminate wasteful discussions on whether value can be increased only by a decrease in price—a much established myth in many marketing circles. The numbers between price and image and between image and quality are simple correlations indicating the degree of association between the two pairs.

The Managerial Component

If all we knew at this point was that quality was more important than either image or price, our task would be extremely difficult. How do we improve quality? If you were assigned the job of improving the quality of your wireless services, where would you start? Without understanding how the market defines quality, this would be a fool's errand. Traditional Six Sigma thinks of quality as the desired specifications of the product. SSM rejects this notion of quality and instead embraces the market's perspective of quality. The relevant aspect of quality is not how it is defined from an engineering perspective but rather how the market defines quality. This is where the managerial component of the model comes into play.

The managerial component identifies the CTQs and their relative importance from the market's perspective. The importance of each CTQ is shown on the left-hand side of the model as numbers adjacent to each CTQ. For example, the most important CTQ is customer focus (.394), followed by technical competence (.361), product features (.148), and billing (.096). How do you improve quality? The answer, in this instance, is to focus on the two CTQs that have the biggest impact: customer focus and technical competence.

OK, so now you are given the task of improving customer focus. What do you do? Customer focus is a particularly broad concept that could include just about anything. However, because the customer focus CTQ was generated using a factor analysis, the market has already defined it. The individual attributes that make up customer focus tell us exactly what the market means:

- Treating your client organization like a valued business partner

- Being responsive to your organization's questions and service needs

- Being a company that consistently delivers above and beyond expectations

- Company reps having a positive attitude

- Company reps promptly making changes to your organization's service when you request them

- Company reps resolving problems to your satisfaction

- After the sale, company reps resolving problems the first time you call

- Company reps accurately representing products and services

- Company reps providing clear and concise explanations about the bill

- Company reps providing timely training on how to use the products and services

- After the sale, the ease with which you can reach the right person to solve your organization's problems

- After the sale, customer service that is easy to do business with

- Being a company that provides business solutions to satisfy all of your organization's communication needs

- Being a company that understands the needs of your business

- Proactive communication on promotions or new product and service offerings

- Providing easy access to products, service, and/or accessories at a convenient retail location

Scanning this list of customer focus attributes reveals tremendous insight into how to go about improving this critical CTQ and ultimately overall quality. The attributes are listed in terms of the importance in defining the customer focus CTQ. The same analysis can be done regarding the technical competence CTQ. Between the two, over 60 percent of the quality component is included.

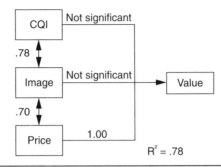

Figure 5.7   Value model for providing electricity to large industrial clients.

Other Examples of Value Models

The value model in Figure 5.7 was generated for a large utility (electrical) serving what it calls its platinum customers—very large industrial clients.

It is included because, as the model illustrates, the only driver of value that was significant was the price factor. Large industrial clients were not dependent on the utility to provide any services except an uninterrupted supply of electricity, and the price of that electricity was all-important. This is a rather unique value model, included to show the specific nature of value within targeted product/markets.

Figure 5.8 captures the VOM for compact tractors sold to estate owners. In this case, quality (CQI) is significantly more important in the value equation (.618) than is price (.281). Image (.101) plays a minor role in how this product/market defines value. Most importantly, looking at the CTQs, the dominant CTQ has to do with the dealer and not the product. This was a point made in an earlier chapter—one that would be missed by those organizations that are strictly product focused. In fact, of the seven CTQs, only three had to do with the prod-

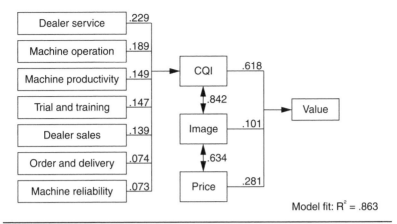

Figure 5.8   Value model for compact tractors.

uct; the rest had to do with either the dealer or the interaction between the manufacturer and the dealer. Put another way, over half of quality is composed of non-product factors. It pays to understand value from the buyer's perspective and not from an internal product-focused vantage.

The Competitive Value Model captures the VOM and provides the information platform for improving operations within the organization. It is the principal and defining tool of the measure stage of the SSM DMAIC paradigm. It goes far beyond the typical market research information that is generated from most market research firms. The Competitive Value Model provides a blueprint for addressing people, product, and process issues that have a direct impact on the organization's competitive value proposition and market share. Subsequent chapters will show how to use this information to identify options for improving people (sales reps), product, and process issues that impact the organization's competitive value proposition and its market share.

FOCUS GROUP

Moderator Guide for Owners of New Manufactured Homes

- How much shopping did you do before deciding on the home you chose? How many dealers did you visit? How far did you travel to visit these dealers? What brands did you consider? Are there any brands that you would simply not consider? Why not?

- Thinking about the dealerships you visited and the salespeople you came into contact with, tell me about the best salespeople you worked with. What did they do that impressed you? Take a few moments and write down these factors. *(List. Our intent here is to create a list of sales attributes that we can use in the quantitative portion of the study. You may have to probe to get specific information regarding the attribute and what it means.)*

- Was there anything about the salespeople that you did not particularly like? Again, take a few moments and write down those aspects of their behavior that you didn't like. *(Again, probe.)*

- What about the dealerships that you visited? What were some of the things you liked about them? Think about which one you liked best (it may not be the one from which you bought your home). What did you like about this dealership? *(List and probe.)*

- What is your opinion concerning the warranty? What elements of it do you like? What elements do you not like?

- What about the dealership(s) that you least liked? What were the things that you didn't like? *(List and probe.)*

- What were the features of the dealership that led you to buy your home from that dealer? Why did you choose that dealer?

- What about the home you purchased? What product features (irrespective of price) were the most important in your decision to purchase the home you did? Which manufacturer do you think makes the best home/RV? Why?

- How did you judge the quality of your home? What features of the home itself can you point to as indicating that the home you purchased is of high quality?

- When you were looking for a home, you probably had certain features or factors in mind. Which of those factors or features were must-haves? In other words, were there any features or factors of the home (dealership) that if missing would have automatically eliminated that model (dealer) from your consideration?

- *Alternative question:* If I were going into business to sell homes, what would I have to do to get you to consider me as a manufacturer? As a dealer?

These two questions are designed to identify what we call "qualifiers."

- What are your expectations about service and after-sale support regarding the dealer from whom you bought your home? How important is the dealer in providing service to you over the time you own the home?

- When you think about the price you paid for your home, what cost aspects did you consider (financing, service, trade-in)?

REFERENCES

Goeke, Reginald, Michael Marx, and Eric Reidenbach. 2008. "Hearing Voices: How Businesses Listen to the Customer." *iSixSigma Magazine*, July/August, 31–38.

Reidenbach, R. Eric. 2009. *The Voice of the Market: Listen, Learn, Lead.* New York: Productivity Press.

The Research Advisors. 2006. www.research-advisors.com.

6

Analyze: Identifying Value Gaps

SSM is all about gaps—value gaps. These gaps underlie the differences in market share. SSM focuses on these gaps in the analysis stage (see Figure 6.1) with an eye to increasing positive gaps between your organization and its competitors or reducing the negative value gaps between your organization and targeted competitors.

To understand the nature of these value gaps, Six Sigma marketers have three unique value-based tools at their disposal: the Competitive Value Matrix, the Customer Loyalty Matrix, and the Competitor Vulnerability Matrix. All of these tools are powered by the Competitive Value Model, discussed in Chapter 5.

These tools inform project identification and provide valuable input into the development of action plans to grow market share. They are instrumental in identifying specific processes for improvement as well as issues regarding people and products, all elements of value delivery. Within the competitive planning process, these tools provide the analysis that informs the competitive analysis, opportunity identification, objectives, and strategy steps of the process.

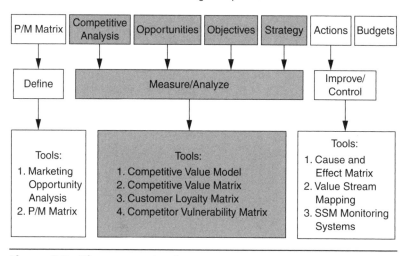

Figure 6.1   The measure/analyze stages.

THE COMPETITIVE VALUE MATRIX

The Competitive Value Matrix displays the competitive value propositions of key competitors within the targeted product/market. The product/market defines the competitive arena, and the Competitive Value Matrix displays the competitive landscape on the basis of how the market perceives these competitors. It is the organization's value radar screen. Figure 6.2 shows the Competitive Value Matrix for the wireless telecom company, XYZ, discussed in Chapter 5.

Quality, in the form of the CQI, is shown on the vertical axis and price on the horizontal axis. The four quadrants are formed by the market averages of quality scores and price scores.

The upper right-hand quadrant is "Outstanding value," so named because it is home to those competitors providing superior quality at a superior price (a price that is evaluated as highly competitive and fair). This is the very definition of value. Companies located within this quadrant are likely to enjoy market

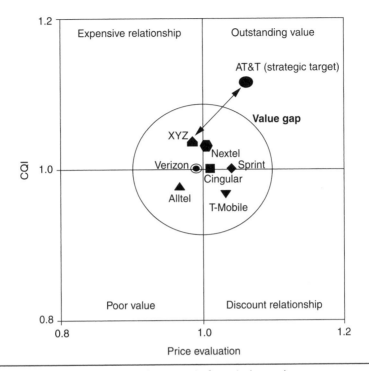

Figure 6.2   Competitive Value Matrix for wireless telecom competitors.

share gains and positive changes in revenue. Only one competitor, AT&T, is located within this quadrant. It is the value leader as well as the market share leader in this product/market.

In the lower left-hand quadrant are the poor value competitors. The market judges them to be providing inferior quality at an inferior price (noncompetitive and unfair). Companies located within this quadrant cannot sustain this position for any length of time. Their poor value status is a leading indicator of declining market share.

The upper left-hand quadrant is "Expensive relationship"; companies located here provide superior quality but at an inferior price. The evaluation of price may be either based on fact or subject to a perceptual distortion. Their strategic task is to move to the right by changing their price evaluation while maintaining their strong quality posture.

Finally, those companies located within the lower right-hand quadrant are the discount relationship companies based on evaluations of inferior quality but a satisfactory price. This is the entry point for many new competitors within an established market. Their task is to improve their quality while maintaining a favorable price evaluation. The Japanese auto industry, Kubota tractors, and Mahindra tractors are examples of companies that have entered the market in this position and have moved or are in the process of moving to the "Outstanding value" quadrant.

In this example, AT&T is the value leader as well as the market share leader. The companies clustered in the circle are undifferentiated when it comes to value. Their value positions are not statistically significant from one another on the quality component or the price component—hence the lack of differentiation. For these companies, the market is shouting, "It doesn't matter who you do business with; they all have the same quality at the same price." This is the commodity quicksand that mires so many organizations in undifferentiated value and mediocre or poor performance. The difference between AT&T and XYZ is the value gap or value advantage that AT&T has over XYZ. The value gap is the focal point of this part of the analysis stage of SSM. AT&T's strategic opportunity is to increase this gap, while XYZ's is to decrease the gap.

UNDERSTANDING VALUE GAPS

For the moment, let's look at this gap from the perspective of XYZ. How does XYZ challenge the value dominance of AT&T? Figure 6.3 reproduces the Competitive Value Model on which this difference is based.

The two key CTQs are customer focus and technical competence. They are significantly and substantially more impor-

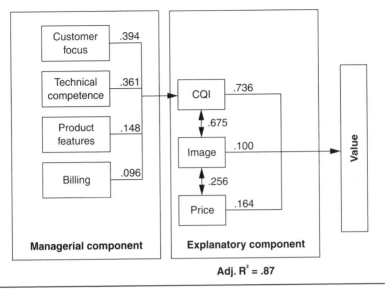

Figure 6.3   Competitive Value Model: Wireless telecom.

tant than price. Moreover, experience shows that a noticeable improvement in quality leads to a positive change in the price component. This occurs because at the current price, customers will get a higher-quality product or service, making the price more justifiable.

Closing the gap will require first identifying the gaps between XYZ and AT&T at the CTQ level. How significant are these gaps and what are they based on? This is shown in Figure 6.4.

The CTQs are listed in the first column. Adjacent to them are the importance weights taken directly from the Competitive Value Model (Figure 6.3). Next are the CTQ scores for each of the competitors. These scores are means on a 10-point performance scale, where 10 is "outstanding performance" and 1 is "poor performance." In SSM, strategy is based on identifying a target competitor—in this case AT&T. Recall from Chapter 3 that XYZ has four strategy options: It can lead, challenge,

CTQ factors	Importance	XYZ	Alltel	AT&T	Sprint	Cingular	Nextel	T-Mobile	Verizon	Gap	Gap importance
Customer focus	0.39	7.64	6.77	8.45	7.08	7.11	7.48	6.95	7.03	0.81	0.32
Technical competence	0.36	7.16	7.28	7.60	7.31	7.36	7.15	7.20	7.67	0.44	0.16
Product features	0.15	8.08	7.41	7.90	7.74	7.71	8.00	7.59	7.95	0.00	0.00
Billing	0.10	8.05	7.36	8.09	7.95	7.83	7.53	7.52	7.20	0.00	0.00

XYZ advantage	XYZ parity	XYZ disadvantage

Figure 6.4   CTQ gap analysis.

follow, or niche. Since AT&T is the leader, XYZ is forced to choose from the remaining three options.

Currently, XYZ is at a disadvantage to AT&T on the two main CTQs. The actual score gap is shown in the next to last column on the right-hand side of the table. This is simply the difference between XYZ's performance score and AT&T's. The "Gap importance" column is the weighted difference, calculated by multiplying the gap by CTQ importance. Gap importance is a function of not only the actual score difference on the CTQ but also the importance of that score. In this case, because there is little difference in the importance of the two CTQs, the relative position regarding gap importance does not change. This is not always the case. XYZ strategy will focus on improving its performance on customer focus and technical competence to challenge AT&T's value superiority, and the gap importance score reveals which performance change will have the greatest impact on XYZ's competitive value proposition. Notice that the gap importance for "Product features" and "Billing" is zero. This is because there is no statistical difference in score in these two CTQs. In other words, the gap is zero.

Let's look at this from the perspective of AT&T. Its value dominance is significant and would result in pats on the back and choruses of "How great we art" in many organizations. That is shortsighted. AT&T is in the position to leverage its dominance, its gap advantage, by investing more heavily to enhance its performance on the two CTQs driving this advantage. In other words, how does AT&T become even more customer focused and technically competent? This will have the effect of creating an even greater gap and enhancing its market share position.

At this juncture the analysis has brought focus squarely on the two CTQs driving the difference between XYZ and AT&T. How the gaps are attacked is the subject of Chapter 7, where more conventional Six Sigma methodology is used to identify projects and improve performance on the key processes involved in delivering improved customer focus and technical competence. Before this is discussed, two other tools that will inform improvements are detailed. Both inform the analysis stage of SSM.

THE CUSTOMER LOYALTY MATRIX

Market share is a function of three factors: retaining current customers, increasing the buying rate of current customers, and acquiring new customers. The first two factors should be addressed prior to developing an aggressive program of customer acquisition. Getting your own house in order and strengthening the loyalty of your customer base is the best place to start. The principal tool for driving this initiative is the Customer Loyalty Matrix, shown in Figure 6.5.

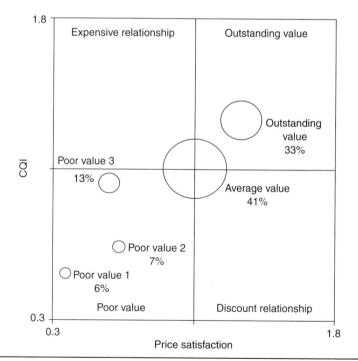

Figure 6.5 The Customer Loyalty Matrix.

The Customer Loyalty Matrix is similar to the Competitive Value Matrix with one exception: Instead of locating companies or brands on the matrix, groups of customers (circles) are placed on the matrix. This placement is based on the similarity in their scores on the two key drivers of value, quality (CQI) and price, using a grouping technique called cluster analysis. The size of the circles reflects the relative size of the group of customers.

In the case of XYZ, only 33 percent of its customer base is receiving the kind of outstanding value that makes them loyal customers. A full 41 percent of its customer base is receiving average value, a level of value that customers can get just about anywhere else. (If you are not clear on this, refer back to the Competitive Value Matrix and the set of undifferentiated average wireless competitors.) These customers are passive shoppers ready to make a move to another supplier when the opportunity arises. Of even worse news to XYZ is that the remainder of its customer base (26 percent) is getting various levels of poor value from XYZ. These are the least loyal customers, and they will actively shop for another option when their contracts expire. They are out there in the marketplace telling others about your poor value and that your services are not worth it! Poor value group 3, comprising 13 percent of XYZ's base, indicates they are receiving a little less than average value and low price satisfaction. Poor value group 2, which comprises about 7 percent of XYZ's customer base, indicates they are receiving very poor quality and poor price satisfaction, while poor value group 1 (about 6 percent of the customer base) indicates they are receiving exceptionally poor quality and price satisfaction.

What are the consequences of this poor value? Figure 6.6 profiles these value groups to explain the implications of value failure and the rewards of delivering outstanding value.

To understand the implications that value has on loyalty and associated outcome measures, compare the scores of the outstanding value group with those of the groups receiving lesser value. There is a consistent and significant drop in scores

Loyalty measure	Value group					
	Poor value group 1	Poor value group 2	Poor value group 3	Average value group	Outstanding value group	
	6%	**7%**	**13%**	**41%**	**33%**	
Overall image of XYZ[1]	4.00	5.00	7.37	7.74	9.04	
Overall network/call quality of XYZ[1]	2.64	4.38	7.45	6.85	8.93	
Overall customer service quality of XYZ[1]	3.17	4.00	6.04	7.32	8.88	
Willingness to recommend XYZ[2]	2.00	2.88	3.87	4.12	4.73	
Likelihood of switching from XYZ[2]	2.17	2.50	3.81	3.72	4.47	
Likelihood of switching for a 10% price reduction[2]	2.00	2.14	3.23	3.06	3.87	
Likelihood of switching for a 20% price reduction[2]	1.54	2.00	2.55	2.54	3.29	
Willingness to renew contract with XYZ[2]	2.15	3.13	4.00	3.98	4.58	

[1] 10-point scale. The higher the score, the more positive the response.
[2] 5-point scale. The higher the score, the less likelihood of switching.

Figure 6.6 Profile of value groups.

on image, network/call quality, customer service performance, and willingness to recommend. Poor network/call quality and poor customer service may, in fact, be causes of the poor value evaluations. Of particular note is the likelihood of switching. The outstanding value group is significantly and substantially less likely to switch than its lower-value counterparts, even under conditions of lower competitive price offerings. They are much more loyal, and this loyalty translates into a greater willingness to renew their contracts with XYZ and recommend it as a carrier. The effects of less than outstanding value delivery are pernicious, causing share erosion from within.

The consequences of this value failure are made evident in Figure 6.7, which reveals the usage and economic impacts of value.

Because all three poor value groups are made up of active shoppers who are most likely to switch, the economic consequences of their switching is disastrous. The potential revenue

	Poor value group 1	Poor value group 2	Poor value group 3	Average value group	Outstanding value group
Average number of units	7.77	17.02	16.08	8.56	6.92
Average cell usage/unit	77 min.	61.5 min.	50 min.	64.4 min.	47.8 min.
Average billed revenue/ unit/year	749.56	930.07	652.41	728.08	683.96
Average total cost/unit	$44.45	$46.96	$41.92	$45.48	$41.77
Estimated average margin/unit	$18.02	$30.54	$12.45	$15.19	$15.23

Figure 6.7 Usage and economic value of value groups.

loss to XYZ is enormous. To calculate the revenue that is in jeopardy, simply multiply the size of the total customer base by the percentage in each value group and then multiply this number by the averaged billed revenue/unit/year or the estimated average margin/unit that is in jeopardy. The cost of poor value gets the attention of management every time.

Changing this situation requires understanding what is underlying these value positions. Figure 6.8 starts this analysis by profiling the value groups based on their CTQ scores.

These are mean scores based on a 10-point scale, with 10 anchored with "excellent performance" and 1 "poor performance." A familiar pattern emerges in the scores. At the basis of these poor value evaluations are the corresponding poor performance scores on the two main CTQs. Any attempt to firm up loyalty will require addressing these CTQs, especially customer focus and technical competence because of their importance.

Again, by way of illustration, breaking the customer focus CTQ into its constituent component attributes provides important insight into loyalty enhancement. These attribute scores, which are mean scores on the 10-point performance scale, are shown in Figure 6.8. Improvement on the customer focus CTQ will require focusing on the individual attributes (see Figure 6.9) with an eye to improving performance on the people, product, and process issues.

	Outstanding value group	Average value group	Poor value group 1	Poor value group 2	Poor value group 3
Customer focus	8.37	5.95	3.67	3.42	2.13
Technical competence	8.21	6.32	4.25	4.21	3.92
Product features	7.93	5.82	4.96	4.75	4.32
Billing	8.16	6.45	5.27	5.18	4.87

Figure 6.8   Profile of value groups based on CTQ scores.

	Outstanding value group	Average value group	Poor value group 1	Poor value group 2	Poor value group 3
Treating your client organization like a valued business partner	9.26	7.53	8.12	4.66	2.97
Being responsive to your organization's questions and service needs	9.36	7.02	5.89	4.32	3.01
Being a company that consistently delivers above and beyond expectations	8.47	8.85	8.01	4.73	2.82
Company reps having positive attitude	9.48	8.68	8.85	4.69	2.00
Company reps promptly making changes to your organization's service when you request them	9.26	7.32	5.89	4.58	3.12
Customer reps resolving problems to your satisfaction	8.98	6.79	5.52	4.12	2.56
After the sale, company reps resolving problems first time you call	8.12	6.09	5.12	5.01	3.12
Company reps accurately representing products and services	8.23	5.52	4.58	4.29	2.89
Company reps providing clear explanations about the bill	8.01	7.02	5.33	5.05	3.58
Company reps providing timely training on how to use the products and services	9.54	8.85	4.98	4.23	2.85
After the sale, the ease with which you can reach the right person to solve your organization's problems	9.23	8.32	5.11	4.38	3.52
After the sale, customer service that is easy to do business with	8.12	7.02	6.88	6.12	3.85
Being a company that provides business solutions to satisfy all your organization's needs	9.55	7.29	5.36	4.96	4.01
Being a company that understands the needs of your business	8.25	7.05	5.67	5.01	3.95
Proactive communications on promotions or new products and service offerings	9.59	7.05	4.98	4.21	3.25
Providing easy access to products, services, and/or accessories at a convenient retail location	8.27	7.96	5.44	4.56	4.01
Renewing contracts is a fair and simple process	8.52	7.53	5.66	4.66	3.64

Figure 6.9 Customer focus attributes by value group.

Another level of analysis is to identify any systematic issues related to poor performance on these CTQs. These systematic factors might include regional differences, new acquisitions with unmerged cultures, poor sales training, distribution factors (different middlemen, different channels), different production facilities, and so forth. The point is, instead of treating these problems as unrelated, there might be some underlying factor causing them. Identifying this systematic problem provides fertile application of Six Sigma methodology. The Customer Loyalty Matrix provides the information to address two aspects of market share: customer retention and increasing the usage rates of current customers.

THE COMPETITOR VULNERABILITY MATRIX

Acquiring new customers is the third element of market share and is addressed by using the Competitor Vulnerability Matrix. New customers will come from either new entrants to the market or prying customers away from competitors, typically a more costly endeavor. In many mature industries, new entrants are few and far between. Acquisition comes primarily from providing superior value that lures competitors' customers to your organization. Conversely, the failure of a competitor to provide sufficient value makes this acquisition effort more efficient and effective if you understand the basis of this failure. That is the purpose of the Competitor Vulnerability Matrix, shown in Figure 6.10.

The Competitor Vulnerability Matrix is similar to the Customer Loyalty Matrix with one exception: Instead of plotting groups of your customer base on the matrix, groups of a competitor's customers (in this case, AT&T) are located in the various quadrants.

AT&T has a particularly loyal customer base, especially when compared to XYZ. There are two groups of outstanding

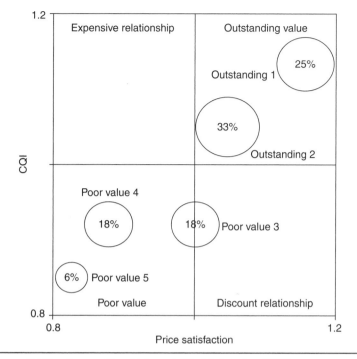

Figure 6.10 Competitor Vulnerability Matrix for AT&T.

value customers: one that includes 25 percent of AT&T's customer base and one that includes 33 percent. In all, 58 percent of its customers have indicated that they are receiving outstanding value from AT&T. These are the most loyal customers and the least likely to switch to a competitor. It would be a waste of time to attempt to attract these customers.

Instead, attention should be directed to the two major groups of poor value customers, poor value groups 3 and 4 again, by focusing on the two major CTQs, customer focus and technical competence. A similar process of decomposing CTQ scores into constituent attribute scores will inform the strategy of attracting AT&T's vulnerable customers. Acquisition strategies formulated around sales programs or promotion programs (communication) can be particularly effective in targeting these poor value customers.

These value tools provide SSM with a powerful analytic capability. These analysis tools inform the identification of opportunities, objectives, and strategy. Their power flows additionally from their ability to identify Six Sigma projects as well as to identify other people and product issues. Much of the value in the wireless telecom example is delivered to the marketplace by means of processes. The customer focus CTQ depends heavily on the sales process, the customer service process, and the customer training process. This is a strength of SSM in both its ability to identify process-related issues and its ability to provide a means for addressing them.

7

Improve: Closing/Growing Value Gaps

The attention of Chapter 6 was on gaps—value gaps and how to analyze them. Value gaps are unique to SSM. They form the basis of the strategy development of SSM and provide the linkage to value creation and value delivery systems that underscore the organization's competitive value proposition. Improve and control flow directly from the action plans in the competitive planning process (see Figure 7.1).

This chapter outlines a data-driven methodology for linking the gap information to value streams and processes, as well as people and products, and identifying Six Sigma projects for improvement, making changes, and developing control mechanisms to monitor the effectiveness of the changes. Improve and control are two sides of the same coin. The improve stage of SSM uses a modified Cause and Effect Matrix, a tool that is well known to the Six Sigma community. Where the more traditional Cause and Effect Matrix is often used as a brainstorming tool and not based on any hard data, the SSM Cause and Effect Matrix is. It is not a brainstorming tool but rather a tool that provides a direct link from the VOM to specific value streams, processes, people, and product issues that identify specific projects for enhancing the organization's competitive value proposition.

Referring back to the *iSixSigma* survey of Six Sigma practitioners (Goeke, Marx, and Reidenbach 2008), another major challenge cited was how to use the VOC in general and how to

SSM: An integrative process

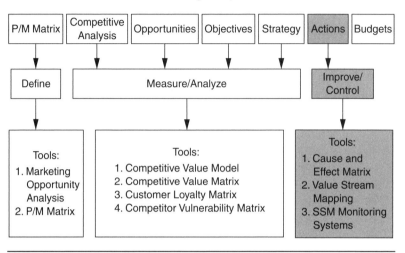

Figure 7.1 The improve/control stages.

link the VOC to internal processes. Comments such as the following characterized this challenge:

- Right translation of VOC/VOM into operational actions

- Translating customer complaints/comments into actionable improvements in our processes

- Translating customer requirements to product/service quality attributes

SSM has a specific tool designed to link the VOM and the VOC to specific value streams and their constituent processes.

VALUE STREAMS AND PROCESSES

Many discussions of Six Sigma treat value streams and processes as synonymous. In keeping with SSM's market focus, SSM makes a crucial distinction: *A value stream is the comprehensive set of activities and information flows that collectively create and deliver value to the customer. A value stream begins with a customer need for a product or service and ends with the customer receiving the product or service and the inherent value.* They are made up of several interconnected processes and involve any number of functional areas within the organization. The critical difference between a value stream and a process is that the value stream exists solely to deliver value to an *external customer*, the one whose perception of value drives revenue and market share increases. Processes, on the other hand, may serve only so-called internal customers such as accounting, interdepartmental transfers, IT services, and so forth.

There are a limited number of value streams within the organization. They might include:

- Order to delivery

- Parts sales to customers

- Service (repair, technical inquiries, and so forth)

Some organizations may have only one value stream. For example, a fast-food restaurant or a tattoo parlor has an order-to-delivery value stream. More complex operations, such as those common to manufacturing, may have more than one.

THE LINKAGE CHALLENGE

One of the more vexing challenges facing the Six Sigma community is the ability to link the VOM or the VOC to specific processes. How, then, does the VOM reach those critical processes where value creation and value delivery occur? Absent the direct linkage, changes are made in response to guesses, agendas, and other non-market-based information. In the absence of this linkage, changes in these value streams and processes are effected on the basis of agenda and guessing. Figure 7.2 outlines the linkage process.

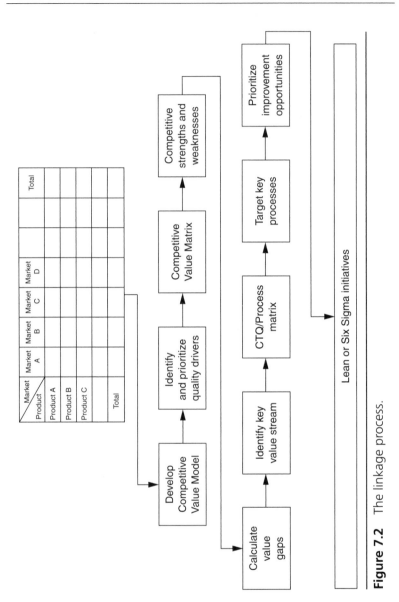

Figure 7.2 The linkage process.

The process begins by using the information captured in the Competitive Value Model described in the measure stage of the DMAIC process (Chapter 5). This is the VOM, which identifies the CTQs. The model prioritizes these CTQs in the order of their importance to the market's definition of value. This is important because focusing on an unimportant CTQ—one that has no ability to move the value dial—is a waste of resources.

The Competitive Value Matrix (Chapter 6) identifies the gap that exists between your organization and the targeted competitor. Again, this may be a positive value gap or a negative value gap. If positive, you will want to leverage this gap advantage and build on it by improving the basis of the gap. This will form the basis of a leadership strategy. If negative, you will want to close it. Closing the gap is fundamental to a challenger or follower strategy. Some gaps will be more important than others not only because of the size of the gap but also because of the importance of the CTQ for which the gap pertains. These gaps can then be prioritized in terms of their impact on the organization's competitive value proposition, linked to a value stream and then linked to specific processes that compose the value stream. This allows the Six Sigma marketer to identify and target those processes having the most impact on the organization's value creation and value delivery systems. This process ensures that subsequent organizational changes—whether they are people, product, or process changes—are made in response to the VOM and not some internal agenda.

LINKING THE VOM TO SPECIFIC VALUE STREAMS AND PROCESSES

An illustration will make the process even more clear, especially when set within an actual case example. XYZ, the wireless telecom company discussed earlier, is regionally focused but competes against a number of national competitors. It is a business-to-business company with no focus on individual customers and relies heavily on direct selling with few retail outlets. Its product/market focus is wireless service/metro markets. For several years the company has been measuring satisfaction and has enjoyed solid satisfaction scores, even though its market share was constant or, more recently, declining. Its churn rate hovered around 50 percent per year, making its unofficial strategy one based on "outselling churn." Like the Queen of Hearts in Wonderland, it was forced to run faster and faster simply to stay in place. This strategy placed an overwhelming weight on selling, so much so that, internally, salespeople became known as headhunters. Their job was to sign up as many customers as they could. Achieving market share goals became extremely problematic. Moreover, there was a problem in the delivery of the handsets to the businesses XYZ served. While for many of the competitors the delivery time was measured in hours, for XYZ it was measured in days. There was some concern as to whether it was qualifying for business based on this long delivery time. In other words, XYZ was losing sales up front as soon as the customer found out that the company might not be able to install the system as soon as the customer wished.

Management recognized the problems they faced and one of the first changes was to switch from a satisfaction metric to a customer value metric. This produced the model shown in Figure 7.3.

The CTQs are prioritized in terms of the order of their importance to value. The model was then translated into the Competitive Value Matrix shown in Figure 7.4, indicating a significant value gap between XYZ and AT&T.

For XYZ the challenge was to close this gap. This closure process began with calculating both the nature and the size of the gap at the CTQ level and at the individual attribute level (Figure 7.5). By way of reminder, the numbers in the matrix

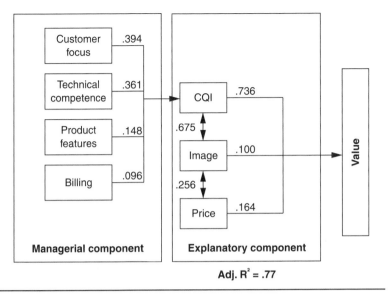

Figure 7.3 Value model: Wireless telecom.

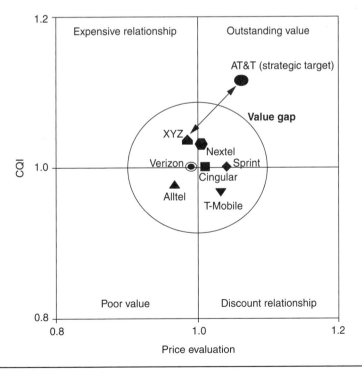

Figure 7.4 Competitive Value Matrix: Wireless telecom.

CTQ factors	Importance	XYZ	Alltel	AT&T	Sprint	Cingular	Nextel	T-Mobile	Verizon	Gap	Gap importance
Customer focus	0.39	7.64	6.77	8.45	7.08	7.11	7.48	6.95	7.03	0.81	0.32
Technical competence	0.36	7.16	7.28	7.60	7.31	7.36	7.15	7.20	7.67	0.44	0.16
Product features	0.15	8.08	7.41	7.90	7.74	7.71	8.00	7.59	7.95	0.00	0.00
Billing	0.10	8.05	7.36	8.09	7.95	7.83	7.53	7.52	7.20	0.00	0.00

XYZ advantage	XYZ parity	XYZ disadvantage

Figure 7.5   Value gaps at the CTQ level.

represent mean scores on a 10-point performance scale, where 1 is poor performance and 10 is excellent performance.

Figure 7.5 identifies customer focus and technical competence as the main CTQs. There is no difference between XYZ's scores and AT&T's scores on product features and billing; they are at parity (no significant statistical differences). Moreover, their relative importance is half or more than half of the first two CTQs. The gap importance is calculated, which directs focus on the key CTQs and key CTQ attributes that will guide the improve stage.

At the attribute level (Figure 7.6), the same process is applied. Again, by way of review, the attributes that make up the CTQ customer focus are listed in the left-hand column. Their relative importance to the CTQs is shown in the second column. Mean performance scores for each of the competitors are contained in the next five columns. Since AT&T is the target, the gap scores are the difference between XYZ's scores and AT&T's. Finally, gap importance, which is the product of the importance of the attribute score and the gap score, is contained in the last column.

The gap analysis has shown that the two CTQs for focus are customer focus and technical competence. Decomposing the customer focus CTQ into its constituent attributes shows which of these attributes are the most important. These are the outputs that we want to change. They are the market's evaluation of XYZ's performance on these attributes. To change its competitive value proposition and ultimately its market share, XYZ must change how it performs on each of these key attributes.

The next step is to identify the different value streams that make up XYZ's value creation and value delivery system. There are two:

- Order/activation/delivery
- Service utilization

Customer focus attributes	Importance	XYZ	Alltel	AT&T	Nextel	Verizon	Gap	Gap importance
Valued business partner	0.82	7.88	6.71	8.45	7.46	6.81	-0.57	-0.47
Responsive to service needs	0.79	7.98	6.83	9.23	7.56	7.30	-1.25	-0.99
Delivering above and beyond expectations	0.72	7.36	6.05	8.75	7.13	6.97	1.39	1.00
Company reps with positive attitude	0.69	8.18	7.61	8.28	8.17	7.44	0.00	0.00
Reps make prompt changes	0.69	7.52	6.56	7.56	7.50	6.22	0.00	0.00
Reps resolving problems	0.82	7.88	6.63	8.99	7.52	6.77	-1.11	-0.91
After the sale, resolving problems first time	0.82	7.44	6.30	8.88	7.22	6.60	-1.44	-1.18
Reps accurately representing products	0.75	7.84	7.18	7.99	7.78	7.45	0.00	0.00
Reps providing clear explanations	0.72	7.60	7.35	7.70	7.73	6.65	0.00	0.00
Reps providing timely training	0.78	7.32	6.07	9.21	6.50	6.81	-1.89	-1.47
After the sale, reaching the right person	0.86	7.59	6.46	9.24	7.21	7.02	-1.65	-1.42
After the sale, easy to do business with	0.79	8.10	7.09	9.28	7.57	7.44	-1.18	-0.93
Providing business solutions	0.80	7.43	7.11	9.18	7.64	7.15	-1.75	-1.40
Understands your needs	0.65	7.81	6.98	7.88	7.78	7.24	0.00	0.00
Proactive communications on new products	0.45	6.79	5.73	7.00	7.39	6.86	0.00	0.00
Providing easy access to product—retail	0.72	7.57	7.54	7.70	7.77	8.13	0.00	0.00

Figure 7.6   Value gaps at the attribute level.

Now, consider the nature of XYZ's business. The customer initiates contact to buy a wireless system, and it is activated and delivered—all part of one value stream. Clearly, there are subprocesses that make up this value stream, such as the sales process, customer training, the order process, the activation process, credit checking, and the delivery process. From the customer's perspective, all these processes take place at the same time (or should)—hence one value stream. Once the customer is using the system there may be inquiries regarding equipment usage. This is captured in the service utilization value stream.

The SSM Cause and Effect Matrix provides the linkage from the VOM's performance evaluation to the individual processes that make up the order/activation/delivery value stream. This is shown in Figure 7.7.

Across the top of the matrix are the individual attributes (*Y*s) that make up the customer focus CTQ. On the left-hand side of the matrix are listed attribute importance and the different processes that make up the order/activation/delivery value stream. The attribute importance score indicates how important each attribute is to the CTQ. These are obtained by either using the factor loadings of the attributes on each CTQ or correlating each attribute with the CTQ. The attributes represent the *Y*s, or the factors that the organization wants to change. Changing the market's evaluation of the organization's performance changes the organization's competitive value proposition and its market share. These attributes are like a report card, indicating the organization's ability to provide value to the market. To change these performance evaluations, the organization must understand the dynamics that drive this performance. In other words, it must identify the people, product, and process issues that impact this performance.

The numbers in the matrix adjacent to each process (*X*s) indicate the impact that each process has on the attribute's

Attribute importance	Valued business partner 0.82	Responsive to service needs 0.79	Delivering above and beyond expectations 0.72	Company reps with positive attitude 0.69	Reps make prompt changes 0.69	Reps resolving problems 0.82	After the sale, resolving problems the first time 0.82	Reps accurately representing products 0.75	Reps providing clear explanations 0.72	Reps providing timely training 0.78	After the sale, reaching the right person 0.86	After the sale, easy to do business with 0.79	Providing business solutions 0.80	Understands your needs 0.65	Proactive communications on new products 0.45	Provides easy access to product—retail 0.72	Process importance
Sales	6	3	6	9	3	3	0	9	9	0	0	0	9	9	9	6	57.0
Delivery	3	3	6	3	0	0	0	0	0	0	3	3	0	0	0	0	16.2
Training	3	0	6	3	0	0	0	3	9	9	3	6	9	9	3	0	46.3
Invoicing	3	0	3	0	0	6	6	0	0	0	6	6	3	6	0	0	30.7

Figure 7.7 Cause and Effect Matrix.

performance. A cross-functional team arrived at these impact numbers by using a simple measuring approach:

0 = no impact

3 = slight impact

6 = moderate impact

9 = heavy impact

Any scale that is easy to understand and easy to apply can be used. For each process, these impacts are captured. They are then multiplied by the attribute importance weight to account for differences in relative importance and then summed. The summated product produces the process importance score on the far right-hand side of the matrix. The higher the score, the more important the process is to the performance of the attributes that make up the customer focus CTQ. This ranking permits the prioritization and the focus of improvement efforts on those processes that will have the greatest impact on enhancing the organization's capacity to deliver superior customer focus. This data-driven approach eliminates internal agendas as the guiding directive in process analysis and reduces the likelihood that the organization will spend resources on efforts that will have marginal or little impact on value enhancement. In this case, the most important process was the sales process (57), followed by training (46.3), invoicing (30.7) and delivery (16.2).

SSM MAPPING

Figure 7.8 captures a map of the two value streams and the individual steps that compose them. While not readable as shown in this figure, suffice to say it illustrates the purpose of using the VOM to identify key areas of concern.

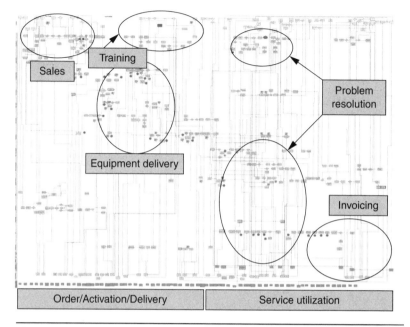

Figure 7.8   Value map.

SSM mapping differs in some respects from the type of mapping done on internal processes that focus on defects and cost reduction. In keeping with its market focus, across the top of the map are the key customer contact points that represent the different types of transactions or events between the customer and the organization. For example, the order/delivery value stream may begin with either a customer inquiry or a contact initiated by a salesperson. Putting in these contact points will produce the basis for developing a skeletal map. Along the sides are the different areas or departments of the organization. Adding in some of the elements of the different processes will help maintain the connectivity and flows within the map. Mapping in too great of detail at this point will not leave time for corrective action.

The map includes a service value stream that was the subject of a subsequent analysis similar to this one but not included in this illustration. The individual processes can be identified on the map where they occur and analyzed in terms of the steps involved in their performance. The Cause and Effect Matrix will tell you the specific processes that need to be mapped in greater detail.

Mapping the sales process the way it actually occurred revealed some interesting insight into other issues. For example, there was no activity regarding training, the number two process. Salespeople were simply trying to close as many deals as they could, causing many unintended customer problems regarding the functioning of the phone system. This problem showed up in the service utilization analysis (problem resolution), where the call center was receiving a preponderance of calls regarding how to use simple features of the phone. In addition, because of the emphasis on sales, orders were submitted that were not properly filled out, resulting in them being sent back to salespeople, who had no economic incentive to properly fill them out. They were not including the necessary information to begin the activation and delivery processes. Salespeople were simply collecting these returned order forms and completing them at their leisure since their principal focus was on creating new accounts as quickly as they could. To them, these were orders they had already put into their "commission column." Customers were led to believe that once the order was taken, they would receive their systems within a short period of time. Not so.

What had initially appeared as a delivery problem was actually a problem resulting from the sales process. The warehouse was not receiving orders, because they had not been attended to by the salespeople. The orders were piling up in a "trouble basket" awaiting further processing. Activations were further delayed because of this problem within the sales process. There is little wonder why the organization was experiencing a 50 percent churn rate with the level of customer focus it was providing customers.

Many changes were made, including providing salespeople with an electronic order form that could not be sent until all necessary information was filled out. This ensured that improperly and inadequately filled-out orders were not being carried around and filled out at the salesperson's leisure. Delivery times dropped from days to hours, and the organization found it was qualifying for more business. In addition, the salespeople underwent further training based on "customer focus" to include an emphasis on training in the use of the system. This reduced the number of calls the call center was receiving. Salespeople were linked to customers at the call center to monitor the quality of the training and to identify areas where training issues still remained. Churn dropped from 50 percent to 30 percent, much more in line with the competition. To reduce this further, XYZ embarked on a lost customer analysis based on its customer loyalty findings. One aspect of this analysis was salient. It was able to institute a selective intervention process based on the economic value of a customer to XYZ. This came from the economic profiling of the different value groups shown in Figure 6.7. Calls from these customers were escalated to supervisors within the call center, and specific interventions were used to keep the customers. As customer loyalty became as important as sales and the sales process was corrected, market share increased significantly.

It's not likely that traditional marketing would have been able to fix the problems facing XYZ by changing elements of the product, promotion (sales), or distribution. It is not likely since the attention would not have been focused on the role that processes played in the creation and delivery of value. This is the strength of SSM.

REFERENCE

Goeke, Reginald, Michael Marx, and Eric Reidenbach. 2008. "Hearing Voices: How Businesses Listen to the Customer." *iSixSigma Magazine*, July/August, 31–38.

8

Control: Monitoring the Competitive Value Proposition and Customer Defects

There are two components to the control stage of the DMAIC process in SSM (see Figure 8.1).

Both elements are focused on monitoring the growth of market share—the overarching goal of SSM. The first has to do with the ongoing monitoring and control of the organization's competitive value proposition. After making changes to the organization's value streams that create and deliver value, it is essential to monitor these changes to ensure that they have the desired impact on the organization's competitive value proposition within the targeted product/market. It makes no sense to make changes to processes, people, or product without a corresponding analysis of those changes.

Contrary to what many think, the organization's competitive value proposition has to be managed. If you are not managing your own value proposition, who is? The answer is your competitors. Making process, people, and product changes is only part of this management process. The other part is monitoring the changes—part of the control stage of SSM.

SSM: An integrative process

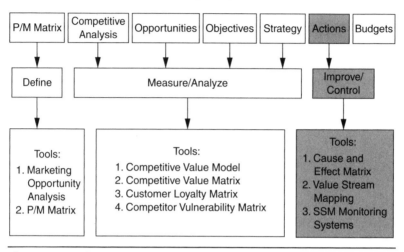

Figure 8.1 The improve/control stages.

Value is relative, and in the absence of a strong management posture, any changes in your competitors' value propositions will negatively impact yours. Your value proposition is a strong buying signal and plays an important role in acquiring new customers—one of the elements of growing market share.

The second component of the control stage has to do with the retention of your current customers. It makes no sense to acquire new customers if there is no active and overt program to keep them. Yet in many organizations, such as in the case of XYZ in Chapter 7, current customers are often taken for granted, and no system exists to monitor their loyalty. Taken together, the acquisition of new customers and the retention of current customers—providing them with an incentive to repurchase, sign new contracts, and recommend your products and services to others—are the drivers of market share. Making sure that this occurs is the focus of the control stage in SSM.

MONITORING YOUR COMPETITIVE VALUE PROPOSITION

Monitoring your competitive value proposition is a market-based initiative. Since value propositions are relative to the different competitors and affected by the competitive dynamics of the targeted product/markets, the control mechanism must have a similar perspective. Again, the Competitive Value Model provides the information platform for this control process. Recall that each CTQ was composed of several attributes that actually defined it. The customer focus CTQ from the wireless telecom example was composed of the following attributes:

- Treating your client organization like a valued business partner

- Being responsive to your organization's questions and service needs

- Being a company that consistently delivers above and beyond expectations

- Company reps having a positive attitude

- Company reps promptly making changes to your organization's service when you request them

- Company reps resolving problems to your satisfaction

- After the sale, company reps resolving problems the first time you call

- Company reps accurately representing products and services

- Company reps providing clear and concise explanations about the bill

- Company reps providing timely training on how to use the products and services

- After the sale, the ease with which you can reach the right person to solve your organization's problems

- After the sale, customer service that is easy to do business with

- Being a company that provides business solutions to satisfy all of your organization's communication needs

- Being a company that understands the needs of your business

- Proactive communication on promotions or new product and service offerings

- Providing easy access to products, service, and/or accessories at a convenient retail location

SSM employs a two-step value proposition monitoring approach. This approach is based on an analogy to medical practice. When an individual is not feeling well, he or she may typically begin with taking his or her temperature. At this point there may be no need for a doctor or more sophisticated assessments. If the temperature is within the proper limits, the individual may simply get a little more rest, buy an over-the-counter remedy, or eat some chicken soup—simple treatments that are less expensive and less complex.

If, however, the individual has an elevated temperature or has more symptoms, he or she might choose to go to a doctor. The doctor will engage in a more sophisticated assessment, for example, a blood test or a more thorough physical exam. This is a more complex and more expensive option.

In SSM, this is exactly how the monitoring of the organization's competitive value proposition operates. It begins with the less complex and less expensive approach. The attributes that make up the customer focus CTQ are listed in descending order of importance to the CTQ. These are the attributes that have the most impact on defining the CTQ. Instead of using the original questionnaire that contained all the attributes, the monitoring questionnaire uses only the top three or four attributes of each CTQ. The questionnaire is fielded in the same way the original one was—that is, surveying not only your organization's customers but also those of your competitors. This abbreviated questionnaire gauges the performance of each competitor and alerts the Six Sigma marketer to any changes in the relative value propositions of the companies competing within the targeted product/market. It is easy, it is inexpensive, and it provides rapid feedback about the competitive situation within the product/market. It is akin to taking the temperature of the patient. There is no need to do a full-scale analysis of the situation at this point.

If, based on monitoring results, the value objectives detailed in your plan are not being achieved, additional changes will be required. These changes may begin with a more detailed analysis using the full value model. If, however, your monitoring results indicate that you are meeting or exceeding your value objectives, further investment to leverage these changes is called for.

Anytime a decline in the organization's competitive value proposition is detected, the full value model questionnaire may be required. This is particularly true if the relative changes are due to competitive changes. Periodic updating of the full value analysis may be required using additional focus groups to identify any new attributes or factors that may have surfaced. Changes in technology, competition, laws, sociocultural factors, or any other exogenous elements may signal the need to update the value model. Updating will take place less often in more mature industries than in those industries that are more volatile.

Using the reduced form questionnaire offers a quick, easy, and less expensive way to control for changes in the competitive dynamics that impact your value proposition. If a further, deeper dive is required, the full value questionnaire can be deployed. This two-stage approach provides greater bang for your buck while providing a strong monitoring effect.

MONITORING CUSTOMER EVENTS

A second monitoring component focuses on the different events or interactions that your customers engage in on a regular basis. These events include the initial sales process, repair service, parts purchases, requests for technical information, and any other type of transaction that takes place between customers and the organization. The goal of monitoring these events is to reduce defects (performance scores of less than 8 on a 10-point scale or whatever score the organization chooses) to less than four per million. Most organizations are probably operating at the 2 or 3 sigma level (around 300,000 bad experiences per one million customer events)—that is, if anyone is actually measuring defects in this manner. SSM seeks to achieve a Six Sigma level regarding customer defects. Unlike the ongoing monitoring system focused on the organization's competitive value proposition, this event monitoring system is focused on the organization's customer base. Its objective is to reduce customer loss and increase loyalty.

Customer events are like rivets on an airplane wing. A plane can lose one or two rivets without any real consequence to its integrity. But at some point, the continued loss of rivets will cause the wing to fail and the plane to crash. Most customers will tolerate event defects up to a point. When that point is reached, they will defect and go elsewhere. Making sure that the customer events are operating properly reduces the potential for customer loss and market share erosion.

Measuring defects at the customer level is significantly more complex than measuring defects in a manufacturing process. The latter operates in a relatively controlled environment, while the former operates in a constantly changing environment over which the organization does not exert significant control. No organization can control how its competitors will operate or how the economy will fare or how the rate of technology changes, to name but a few factors. Add to this the fact that customers are not simple inert lumps of metal to be processed but are constantly changing learning machines.

Accordingly, defects should be measured in terms of the success or failure of the value a customer experiences when he or she transacts with the organization. Are these transactions or events value laden, or are these events creating a value deficit? Customer transactions represent the ultimate test of the organization's everyday ongoing value creation and delivery processes. For this reason they represent both an important issue and metric for any organization.

REQUIREMENTS OF AN EFFECTIVE MONITORING SYSTEM

For the monitoring system to be of value to the organization, it must exhibit several characteristics. First, it must be *event specific*. This means it must be able to focus on the key events that take place in a customer's life cycle. These events include the sales process, customer inquiries regarding billing or technical assistance, parts purchases, service, and any other events indigenous to a specific industry.

Second, the monitoring system must provide *timely results*. Receiving information on a batch basis two months after the event is too late. Third, the monitoring system must be *actionable*. It must provide information that can be acted on. Finally, the system is made even stronger if there is a *"red flag" capability* built into it. If performance on any event is shown to be inferior (defined as a score of 8 or lower or any other predetermined score on a 10-point scale), this defect is brought to the attention of the proper individual in a timely manner. This "red flag" capability provides the opportunity for immediate intervention. The quicker the intervention, the more likely the defect can be repaired.

What follows is an example of an SSM control system that meets all these criteria. It couples a flexible monitoring system with a dashboard, providing clear, up-to-the-moment information regarding the organization's value system.

One of the hallmarks of the system is its ability to track any predefined event. Figure 8.2 shows the opening screen, indicating the date of the survey and allowing the user to choose the event (dealer service, sales process, and so forth), the questions to be included in the survey, the place where the survey is to be administered, the vendor, and the market to be surveyed.

Respondents are recruited from a list of transactions—in this case collected at the dealer level (customer name, type of event, phone number) and sent electronically to the center conducting the surveys. Customer contact information can be

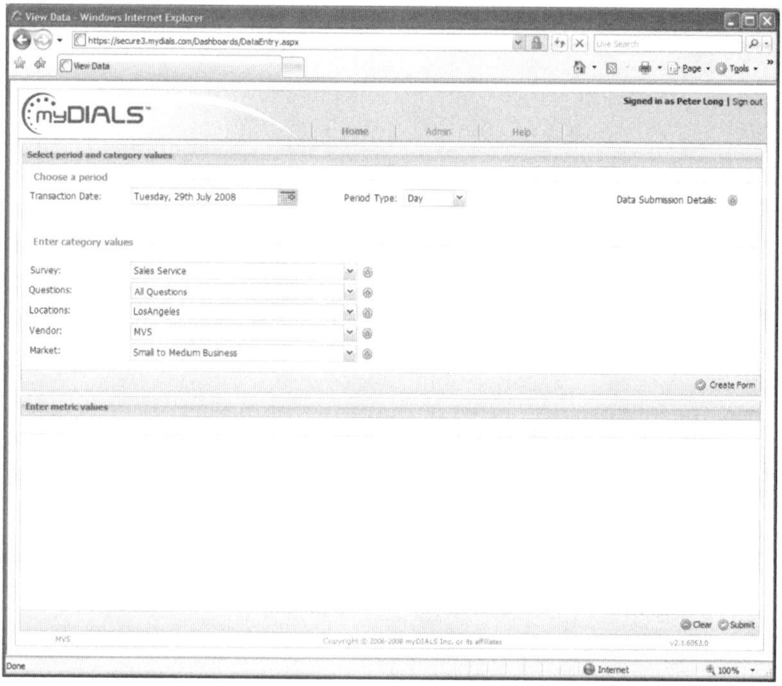

Figure 8.2   Monitoring system: Opening screen.

collected at any level in the distribution system and sent electronically to where the survey is to be conducted. Collecting data in this way, on a daily basis, will produce results that can be made available within one or two working days. The system can also be set up to allow the survey to be conducted at the dealer, branch, broker, or agent level.

A drop-down screen (Figure 8.3) provides information on the customer being interviewed and a check to make sure that the customer is not being over-interviewed. This is important since interviewing the same customer can not only provide misleading information but also become frustrating to the customer. Directions are provided for the interviewer conducting the survey.

Figure 8.4 shows the kinds of questions used, along with the responses from the customer. These questions are taken

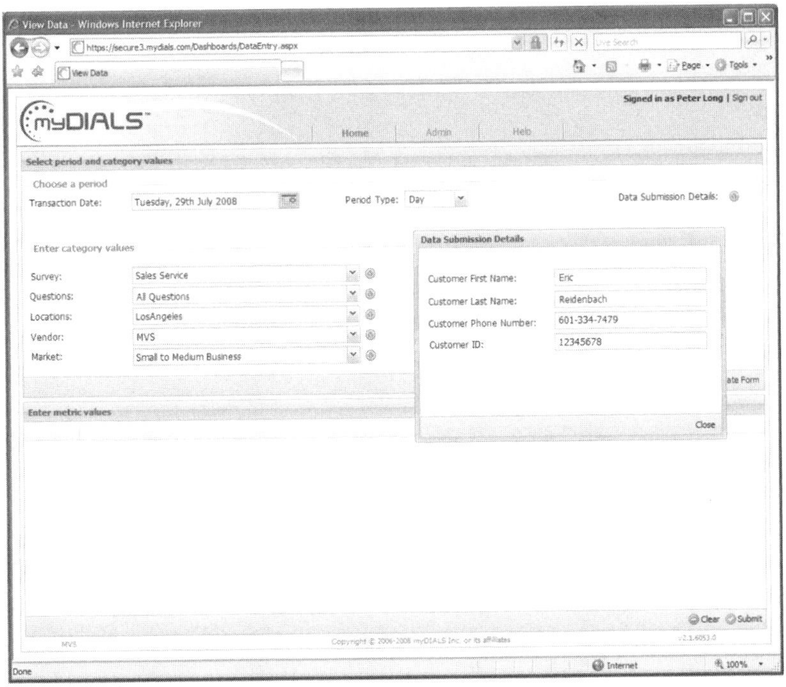

Figure 8.3 Customer information.

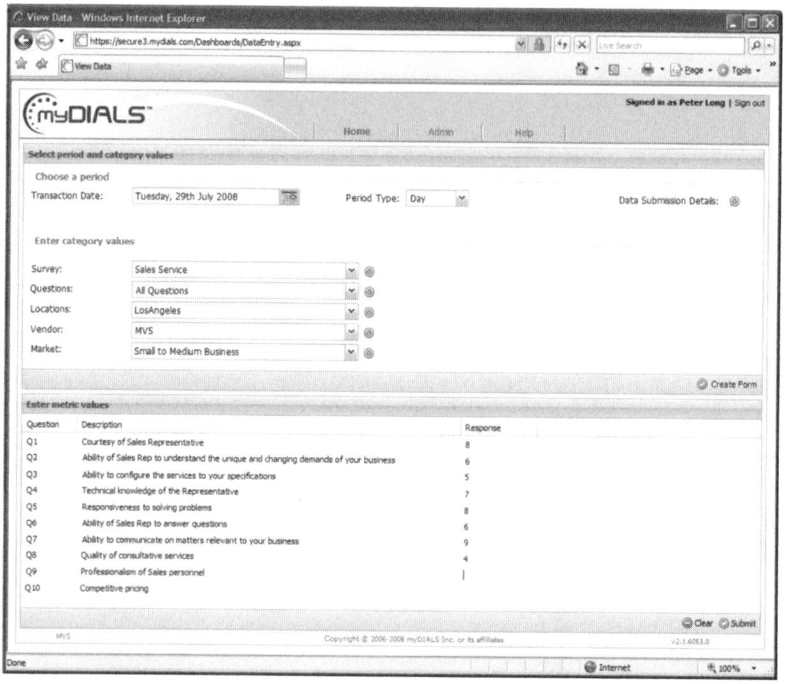

Figure 8.4   Sample monitoring questions.

from the CTQs generated in the value model for this product/ market. Once these responses are collected, they are submitted to a continuously updated data bank for up-to-the-minute analysis.

Some of the analyses are shown in Figure 8.5, where overall responses to the survey questions are shown as well as performance trends and a response Pareto.

Red-flag situations are identified (dealers having knowledgeable parts people), tracked, and used to provide corrective feedback to the appropriate individual. Again, responses can be broken down by location, product/market, date, or any other categorization factor built into the system. This provides a clear, easy to understand summary of what is going on regard-

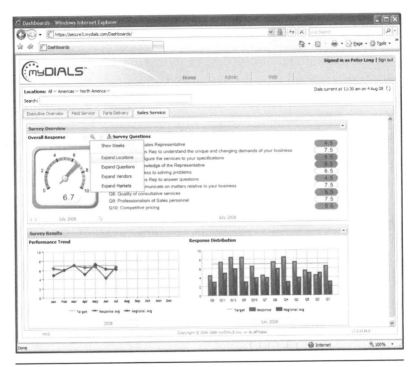

Figure 8.5   Sample analysis of monitoring system.

ing the way in which the organization handles specific types of transactions or customer events.

This type of system permits the electronic communication of results to specific individuals. The information can be rolled up from each dealer, branch, broker, or agent into a regional analysis with comparisons, a corporate level analysis, or information sent back to channel members showing their results compared against a peer group.

How many organizations conducting traditional Six Sigma deployments put in place some sort of control system to monitor the changes made in specific processes? Probably most do on the basis that it makes no sense to make changes without being able to ensure that the changes made are accomplishing what was originally intended. The same argument holds true with regard to SSM activities. Changing people, product, or process issues that impact the organization's value streams, which in turn affects the organization's competitive value proposition (a leading indicator of market share), requires a control function. While somewhat more complex, this monitoring need is no less necessary. It is a critical part of the modified DMAIC approach that underlies the structure of SSM.

9

Deploying SSM

A typical question regarding how to deploy SSM has to do with whether it is better (easier or more effective) to turn Black Belts into marketers or marketers into Black Belts. The answer is neither. To try to do either misses the whole point of SSM. SSM represents a mini paradigm shift, if you will—one that requires a different way of thinking and viewing the way the organization conducts business. Trying to train marketers to be Black Belts infuses them with the traditional approach to Six Sigma that lacks the focus on value and value tools, the role of Six Sigma in the competitive planning process, and the necessary focus on market share growth. Similarly, immersing Black Belts into the methodologies of marketing produces much of the same limiting results. A significant shift in thinking is required of both groups. Figure 9.1 identifies some of the elements of this shift in thinking. While not necessarily exhaustive, it is representative.

With this as a prelude, how can organizations accommodate and nurture the growth of SSM? Or, put another way, what are the surefire ways to doom SSM to an early failure? There are about five or six factors that will affect the adoption and rate of adoption of SSM. Most of these are part and parcel of any change management, but some are worth repeating. Let's begin with the obvious.

Six Sigma ───────►	SSM ◄─────	Marketing
Internal focus	Product/Market focus	Market segment focus
Customer satisfaction	Customer value	Customer satisfaction
Cost/Defect reduction	Revenue/Market share	Revenue/Market share
Quality at production	Quality at consumption	Little quality focus
Product focus	Market focus	Customer focus
Focus on efficiency	Focus on efficiency and effectiveness	Focus on effectiveness
Data driven	Data driven	Agenda (not data) driven
Product defects	Customer event defects	Customer loyalty
Processes	Value streams	4Ps
VOC	VOM	VOC

Figure 9.1 SSM: A confluence of thought.

BUSINESS PHILOSOPHY

Business philosophy refers to the way the organization thinks about the various components that contribute to its success. It reflects an emphasis on the factor (or factors) that management believes contributes to its success and strategic health. In some cases, it is used synonymously with "culture," but it actually represents only a part of the culture.

There are several business philosophies extant in corporate America. They are the result of an adaptation to what business organizations see as the relative importance of exogenous factors affecting their business.

The production or product philosophy has an internal vision of what drives success. It emphasizes the product and the means of producing that product, especially costs. These are typically engineering-dominated organizations that rely heavily on engineering specifications to drive production. Many of them are the enterprises that have bought into the power of Six Sigma to reduce defects and costs. They lack a market focus and do not have well-developed systems for capturing the VOC or the VOM. Managements often argue that they already know everything they need to know about the customer. The challenge for these firms is to shift their view from an internal one to an external one and begin to understand the importance of the market and their ability to react to it in driving the success of their concerns.

There are many organizations that have embraced a selling philosophy. These are firms that place a heavy emphasis on sales, advertising, and other promotional factors. They tend to be somewhat externally focused but believe that the key to success is the ability to sell what they produce rather than what the market wants. Price and price promotions are important tools within this type of enterprise. There is no selling objection that can't be overcome with a price reduction. These organizations confuse pricing problems with value problems. They fail to realize that, in the eyes of the market, the quality of their products or services does not warrant the price they are charging for them. Their products and services aren't worth it. This is the very nature of value, and with all of their focus on selling, the quality side of the issue is ignored. A key to identifying sales-oriented firms is the subordination of marketing to a sales executive rather than the other way around. The challenge for these organizations is to be willing to adopt a more structured and less "artful" approach to business. To many, the adoption of SSM will be seen as an infringement on their knowledge and selling acumen rather than a way to enhance their effectiveness.

Businesses with a market philosophy or focus will already have developed an external focus and may have systems for using the VOC or VOM to drive internal operations. In some respects they may have an easier time in making SSM work, especially if they have a well-established and well-entrenched Six Sigma initiative. These organizations already recognize the importance of the market to their strategic well-being, and this recognition is a critical step. The big challenge is to penetrate the functionalism that underscores their way of doing business and to put in its place an understanding of value and how processes create and deliver value. They typically lack a structured system for approaching the market, again a potentially significant challenge.

For starters, it might be useful for the organization to conduct an audit of its business philosophy. This does not have to be a formal paper and pencil audit but rather one based on conversations with people in the organization. What is important to the organization? Look at the structure—companies' structures reflect what is most important to them. Look at their pay plans. What functions receive the highest compensation? Understanding the philosophy of the organization will provide a starting point for understanding what needs to change. This will point out the specific factors and operating ethos that will be either an impediment or a facilitator of change. Creating the proper environment, one that is receptive to the premise of SSM, provides a fertile incubation chamber for its growth.

TOP MANAGEMENT SUPPORT

Nothing will kill a new initiative faster than lack of top management support. Regardless of the philosophy, top management support will be essential. Change of any sort is likely to be met with some degree of resistance—ranging from complete rejection to a grudging willingness to adapt. Many organizations have poisoned the culture to change with frequent and misapplied "flavor of the month" initiatives—the "cure du jour," if you will.

I have run into a couple of organizations that are run by consensus and have come to believe that to seek consensus is to seek failure. In some consensus-run organizations a single "yeah but" is enough to kill a new initiative. There will always be a need for a leader rather than a herd instinct to run an organization. The success of Six Sigma at GE has been attributed to the leadership strength of Jack Welch. If the leader does not buy into SSM, who will?

At one organization I was part of a team that was developing Customer Value Models for different brands. It was decided that there would be five pilots to determine the value that such a program would offer. As soon as the different brand managers learned of the support from top management, those 5 pilots grew to 12. Everyone wanted to be part of the change.

RESOURCES

Organizations pay for what they value. People who work in organizations know and understand this. Underfunding an initiative sends a clear signal that leadership does not think the initiative is worth it. In other words, there is no value in its deployment. People who work in organizations both know and understand this signal. In order to make SSM work, management must commit the necessary resources to it.

Simply adding SSM to the job description of a Black Belt or a marketing person will not work. Making SSM a part-time job signals the amount of support and dedication the organization has for it. This is a surefire way to doom the initiative to a short life, where it becomes another "flavor of the month"; all people have to do is keep low and it too shall pass.

SSM will place a heavy burden on information needs. Most organizations will not be equipped to provide the necessary information that drives SSM. Once the organization develops a P/M Matrix and identifies all of the relevant competitive arenas in which it chooses to compete, the information needs will become more apparent. Partnering with a reliable data collection supplier will be a long-term plus.

TRAINING

SSM will require a significant amount of training. While many Black Belts have a knowledge of statistics, the type of statistics required in SSM is different. Six Sigma marketers will have to understand the mechanics of multivariate statistics such as factor analysis, cluster analysis, multiple regression analysis, and other techniques. Depending on the amount of outsourcing done, Six Sigma marketers may not have to be experts, but certainly they should be conversant so that they know what to ask for from a supplier and will be able to interpret what they get. Similarly, the transition from a customer satisfaction mentality to a customer value paradigm complete with an understanding of the different value tools is required. Learning how to interpret a Customer Value Model, a Competitive Value Matrix, and the other tools is essential. Value drives everything in SSM and is the core concept.

INCENTIVES

Some organizations are fond of the "burning platform" impetus for change; others are not. What I have found is that people will evaluate change and determine whether it is in their best interest to adapt. To the extent that SSM can be incentivized, it will be adopted much faster. Whether this is a financial incentive tied to a performance evaluation or linked to advancement, a system should be set up that rewards employee engagement. This in turn is a direct function of the support and commitment that the organization has for SSM. For some, change will be difficult, and making it in their best interest to change provides a motivation for sticking with it.

SUCCESS

Nothing sells a change like success. Focusing on doable SSM projects that have an increased probability of success can demonstrate the effectiveness of SSM. Adopt a crawl–walk–run approach to deploying SSM. As success builds, so too will the acceptance of SSM.

No longer is there an excuse for poor quality and poor value. Companies have to actively and knowingly pursue a strategy of creating and delivering poor quality and poor value. Advances in quality management in the form of total quality management (TQM), ISO, Six Sigma, and SSM provide companies with the tools to provide their targeted markets with superior value—one that dominates their competitors.

Even given the universal availability of these tools, some companies will execute more effectively and efficiently than others. It is this execution and the adoption of SSM that will determine who dominates and is rewarded with increased market share and profitability. The differentiating factor is the willingness to adopt these tools, to master them, and then to execute them properly.

Index

Belong to the Quality Community!

Established in 1946, ASQ is a global community of quality experts in all fields and industries. ASQ is dedicated to the promotion and advancement of quality tools, principles, and practices in the workplace and in the community.

The Society also serves as an advocate for quality. Its members have informed and advised the U.S. Congress, government agencies, state legislatures, and other groups and individuals worldwide on quality-related topics.

Vision

By making quality a global priority, an organizational imperative, and a personal ethic, ASQ becomes the community of choice for everyone who seeks quality technology, concepts, or tools to improve themselves and their world.

ASQ is...

- More than 90,000 individuals and 700 companies in more than 100 countries

- The world's largest organization dedicated to promoting quality

- A community of professionals striving to bring quality to their work and their lives

- The administrator of the Malcolm Baldrige National Quality Award

- A supporter of quality in all sectors including manufacturing, service, healthcare, government, and education

- YOU

Visit www.asq.org for more information.

ASQ Membership

Research shows that people who join associations experience increased job satisfaction, earn more, and are generally happier*. ASQ membership can help you achieve this while providing the tools you need to be successful in your industry and to distinguish yourself from your competition. So why wouldn't you want to be a part of ASQ?

Networking

Have the opportunity to meet, communicate, and collaborate with your peers within the quality community through conferences and local ASQ section meetings, ASQ forums or divisions, ASQ Communities of Quality discussion boards, and more.

Professional Development

Access a wide variety of professional development tools such as books, training, and certifications at a discounted price. Also, ASQ certifications and the ASQ Career Center help enhance your quality knowledge and take your career to the next level.

Solutions

Find answers to all your quality problems, big and small, with ASQ's Knowledge Center, mentoring program, various e-newsletters, *Quality Progress* magazine, and industry-specific products.

Access to Information

Learn classic and current quality principles and theories in ASQ's Quality Information Center (QIC), *ASQ Weekly* e-newsletter, and product offerings.

Advocacy Programs

ASQ helps create a better community, government, and world through initiatives that include social responsibility, Washington advocacy, and Community Good Works.

Visit www.asq.org/membership for more information on ASQ membership.

*2008, The William E. Smith Institute for Association Research

ASQ Certification

ASQ certification is formal recognition by ASQ that an individual has demonstrated a proficiency within, and comprehension of, a specified body of knowledge at a point in time. Nearly 150,000 certifications have been issued. ASQ has members in more than 100 countries, in all industries, and in all cultures. ASQ certification is internationally accepted and recognized.

Benefits to the Individual
- New skills gained and proficiency upgraded
- Investment in your career
- Mark of technical excellence
- Assurance that you are current with emerging technologies
- Discriminator in the marketplace
- Certified professionals earn more than their uncertified counterparts
- Certification is endorsed by more than 125 companies

Benefits to the Organization
- Investment in the company's future
- Certified individuals can perfect and share new techniques in the workplace
- Certified staff are knowledgeable and able to assure product and service quality

Quality is a global concept. It spans borders, cultures, and languages. No matter what country your customers live in or what language they speak, they demand quality products and services. You and your organization also benefit from quality tools and practices. Acquire the knowledge to position yourself and your organization ahead of your competition.

Certifications Include
- Biomedical Auditor – CBA
- Calibration Technician – CCT
- HACCP Auditor – CHA
- Pharmaceutical GMP Professional – CPGP
- Quality Inspector – CQI
- Quality Auditor – CQA
- Quality Engineer – CQE
- Quality Improvement Associate – CQIA
- Quality Technician – CQT
- Quality Process Analyst – CQPA
- Reliability Engineer – CRE
- Six Sigma Black Belt – CSSBB
- Six Sigma Green Belt – CSSGB
- Software Quality Engineer – CSQE
- Manager of Quality/Organizational Excellence – CMQ/OE

Visit www.asq.org/certification to apply today!

ASQ Training

Classroom-based Training

ASQ offers training in a traditional classroom setting on a variety of topics. Our instructors are quality experts and lead courses that range from one day to four weeks, in several different cities. Classroom-based training is designed to improve quality and your organization's bottom line. Benefit from quality experts; from comprehensive, cutting-edge information; and from peers eager to share their experiences.

Web-based Training

Virtual Courses

ASQ's virtual courses provide the same expert instructors, course materials, interaction with other students, and ability to earn CEUs and RUs as our classroom-based training, without the hassle and expenses of travel. Learn in the comfort of your own home or workplace. All you need is a computer with Internet access and a telephone.

Self-paced Online Programs

These online programs allow you to work at your own pace while obtaining the quality knowledge you need. Access them whenever it is convenient for you, accommodating your schedule.

Some Training Topics Include
- Auditing
- Basic Quality
- Engineering
- Education
- Healthcare
- Government
- Food Safety
- ISO
- Leadership
- Lean
- Quality Management
- Reliability
- Six Sigma
- Social Responsibility

Visit www.asq.org/training for more information.